Together towards Life

Together towards Life

Mission and Evangelism in Changing Landscapes

with a Practical Guide

Edited by Jooseop Keum

**World Council
of Churches**
Publications

TOGETHER TOWARDS LIFE
Mission and Evangelism in Changing Landscapes
- with a Practical Guide
Edited by Jooseop Keum

WCC Publications is the book publishing programme of the World Council of Churches. Founded in 1948, the WCC promotes Christian unity in faith, witness and service for a just and peaceful world. A global fellowship, the WCC brings together more than 349 Protestant, Orthodox, Anglican and other churches representing more than 560 million Christians in 110 countries and works cooperatively with the Roman Catholic Church.

Cover design: 4 Seasons Book Design/Michelle Cook
Cover image: "Girls Playing in Timbuktu," Paul Jeffrey, with permission
Book design and typesetting: 4 Seasons Book Design/Michelle Cook
ISBN: 978-2-8254-1624-2

World Council of Churches
150 route de Ferney, P.O. Box 2100
1211 Geneva 2, Switzerland
www.oikoumene.org

Contents

Foreword

The new World Council of Churches (WCC) ecumenical affirmation on mission and evangelism, *Together towards Life: Mission and Evangelism in Changing Landscapes*, was prepared by the Commission on World Mission and Evangelism (CWME) and was unanimously approved as an official statement of the WCC by the central committee at its meeting on the island of Crete, Greece, on 5 September 2012. The CWME is thankful to God that the world church and mission bodies of the WCC have been able to reach a common understanding of and commitment to God's mission today. The commission is also grateful that the affirmation is provoking fresh interest in the new vision of ecumenical mission thinking and action.

After the central committee's approval, CWME organized a consultation in January 2013, Kochi, India. The aim was to translate the new concepts brought by the affirmation into missional actions in local congregations, mission organizations and missiological formation. Based on the consultation, *A Practical Guide* on the new statement has been produced by the commission. Therefore, this book consists of three components:

- Part One is the new WCC affirmation on mission and evangelism, *Together towards Life: Mission and Evangelism in Changing Landscapes.*
- Part Two is *A Practical Guide* to the affirmation approved by CWME.

- The third component is a DVD that contains video clips on the history and activities of CWME, the eight preparatory study reports to the new statement, and the centenary issue of the *International Review of Mission* (IRM).

This book is meant to enable reflection, study and application of the new mission statement. Therefore, CWME would like to invite all people who are interested, who are committed to God's mission, to take up the new vision and direction of mission that has been produced by the new mission statement.

I would like to express my sincere gratitude to Metropolitan Dr Geevarghese Mor Coorilos, CWME moderator; to Prof. Kirsteen Kim, vice-moderator; as well as to the commissioners, staff and all the working group members for their tireless and creative work, over the past several years, in developing the new ecumenical statement. My deepest appreciation goes to Rev. Prof. Kenneth Ross, Ms Eva Christina Nilsson and Rev. Dr Roderick Hewitt, who have enormously contributed to and successfully compiled the guide. My special thanks to Mr. Coetzee Zietsman, who produced the CWME videos and edited the DVD. Wiley-Blackwell has kindly given permission to use material from two recent issues of *International Review of Mission,* 100.2 and 101.1, on the DVD.

I hope that this book will inspire churches, mission bodies and practitioners to a renewed commitment to God's mission today and tomorrow. A new milestone is set up! Let us journey together towards life in the mission of the Holy Spirit!

Jooseop Keum
Secretary
Commission on World Mission and Evangelism

Together towards Life: Mission and Evangelism in Changing Landscapes

New Affirmation on Mission and Evangelism

New WCC Affirmation on Mission and Evangelism
Commission on World Mission and Evangelism (CWME)

The Commission on World Mission and Evangelism (CWME) has, since the WCC Porto Alegre assembly in 2006, been working toward and contributing to the construction of a new ecumenical mission affirmation. The new statement will be presented to the WCC 10th Assembly at Busan, Republic of Korea, in 2013. Since the integration of the International Missionary Council (IMC) and the World Council of Churches (WCC) in New Delhi in 1961, there has been only one official WCC position statement on mission and evangelism which was approved by the central committee in 1982, Mission and Evangelism: An Ecumenical Affirmation. *This new mission affirmation was unanimously approved by the WCC central committee on 5 September 2012 at its meeting on the island of Crete, Greece. It is the aim of this new ecumenical discernment to seek vision, concepts and directions for a renewed understanding and practice of mission and evangelism in changing landscapes. It seeks a broad appeal, even wider than WCC member churches and affiliated mission bodies, so that we can commit ourselves together to fullness of life for all, led by the God of Life!*

Together towards Life: Introducing the Theme

1.   We believe in the Triune God who is the creator, redeemer, and sustainer of all life. God created the whole *oikoumene* in God's image and constantly works in the world to affirm and safeguard life. We believe in Jesus Christ, the Life of the world, the incarnation of God's love for the world (John 3:16).[1] Affirming life in all its fullness is Jesus Christ's ultimate concern and mission (John 10:10). We believe in God, the Holy Spirit, the Life-giver, who sustains and empowers life and renews the whole creation (Gen. 2:7; John 3:8). A denial of life is a rejection of the God of life. God invites us into the life-giving mission of the Triune God and empowers us to bear witness to the vision of abundant life for all in the new heaven and earth. How and where do we discern God's life-giving work that enables us to participate in God's mission today?

2.   Mission begins in the heart of the Triune God and the love which binds together the Holy Trinity overflows to all humanity and creation. The missionary God who sent the Son to the world calls all God's people (John 20:21), and empowers them to be a community of hope. The church is commissioned to celebrate life, and to resist and transform all life-destroying forces, in the power of the Holy Spirit. How important it is to "receive the Holy Spirit" (John 20:22) to become living witnesses to the coming reign of God! From a renewed appreciation of the mission of the Spirit, how do we re-envision God's mission in a changing and diverse world today?

3.   Life in the Holy Spirit is the essence of mission, the core of why we do what we do and how we live our lives. Spirituality gives the deepest meaning to our lives and motivates our actions. It is a sacred gift from the Creator, the energy for affirming and caring for life. This mission spirituality has a dynamic of transformation which, through the spiritual commitment of people, is capable of transforming the

---

1. Unless otherwise indicated, Bible quotations are from the New Revised Standard Version (NRSV). Abbreviations used for other translations include KJV (Authorized/King James Version), NIV (New International Version), and REB (Revised English Bible).

world in God's grace. How can we reclaim mission as a transformative spirituality which is life-affirming?

4. God did not send the Son for the salvation of humanity alone or give us a partial salvation. Rather the gospel is the good news for every part of creation and every aspect of our life and society. It is therefore vital to recognize God's mission in a cosmic sense and to affirm all life, the whole *oikoumene*, as being interconnected in God's web of life. As threats to the future of our planet are evident, what are their implications for our participation in God's mission?

5. The history of Christian mission has been characterized by conceptions of geographical expansion from a Christian centre to the "unreached territories," to the ends of the earth. But today we are facing a radically changing ecclesial landscape described as "world Christianity" where the majority of Christians either are living or have their origins in the global South and East.[2] Migration has become a worldwide, multi-directional phenomenon which is reshaping the Christian landscape. The emergence of strong Pentecostal and charismatic movements from different localities is one of the most noteworthy characteristics of world Christianity today. What are the insights for mission and evangelism—theologies, agendas and practices—of this "shift of the centre of gravity of Christianity"?

6. Mission has been understood as a movement taking place from the centre to the periphery, and from the privileged to the marginalized of society. Now people at the margins are claiming their key role as agents of mission and affirming mission as transformation. This reversal of roles in the envisioning of mission has strong biblical foundations because God chose the poor, the foolish, and the powerless (1 Cor. 1:18-31) to further God's mission of justice and peace so that life may flourish. If there is a shift of the mission concept from "mission *to* the margins" to "mission *from* the margins," what then is the distinctive contribution of the people from the margins?

2. See Todd M. Johnson and Kenneth R. Ross eds., *Atlas of Global Christianity* (Edinburgh: Edinburgh University Press, 2009).

And why are their experiences and visions crucial for re-imagining mission and evangelism today?

7.   We are living in a world in which faith in mammon threatens the credibility of the gospel. Market ideology is spreading the propaganda that the global market will save the world through unlimited growth. This myth is a threat not only to economic life but also to the spiritual life of people, and not only to humanity but also to the whole creation. How can we proclaim the good news and values of God's kingdom in the global market or win over the spirit of the market? What kind of missional action can the church take in the midst of economic and ecological injustice and crisis on a global scale?

8.   All Christians, churches, and congregations are called to be vibrant messengers of the gospel of Jesus Christ, which is the good news of salvation. Evangelism is a confident but humble sharing of our faith and conviction with other people. Such sharing is a gift to others which announces the love, grace, and mercy of God in Christ. It is the inevitable fruit of genuine faith. Therefore, in each generation, the church must renew its commitment to evangelism as an essential part of the way we convey God's love to the world. How can we proclaim God's love and justice to a generation living in an individualized, secularized, and materialized world?

9.   The church lives in multi-religious and multi-cultural contexts and new communication technology is also bringing the people of the world into a greater awareness of one another's identities and pursuits. Locally and globally, Christians are engaged with people of other religions and cultures in building societies of love, peace, and justice. Plurality is a challenge to the churches and serious commitment to interfaith dialogue and cross-cultural communication is therefore indispensable. What are the ecumenical convictions regarding common witnessing and practicing life-giving mission in a world of many religions and cultures?

10. The church is a gift of God to the world for its transformation towards the kingdom of God. Its mission is to bring new life and announce the loving presence of God in our world. We must participate in God's mission in unity, overcoming the divisions and tensions that exist among us, so that the world may believe and all may be one (John 17:21). The church, as the communion of Christ's disciples, must become an inclusive community and exists to bring healing and reconciliation to the world. How can the church renew herself to be missional and move forward together towards life in its fullness?

11. This statement highlights some key developments in understanding the mission of the Holy Spirit within the mission of the Triune God (*missio Dei*) which have emerged through the work of CWME. It does so under four main headings:

Spirit of Mission: Breath of Life
Spirit of Liberation: Mission from the Margins
Spirit of Community: Church on the Move
Spirit of Pentecost: Good News for All

Reflection on such perspectives enables us to embrace dynamism, justice, diversity, and transformation as key concepts of mission in changing landscapes today. In response to the questions posed above, we conclude with ten affirmations for mission and evangelism today.

Spirit of Mission: Breath of Life

The Mission of the Spirit

12. God's Spirit—*ru'ach*—moved over the waters at the beginning (Gen. 1:2), being the source of life and the breath of humankind (Gen. 2:7). In the Hebrew Bible, the Spirit led the people of God—inspiring wisdom (Prov. 8), empowering prophecy (Is. 61:1), stirring life

from dry bones (Ezek. 37), prompting dreams (Joel 2), and bringing renewal as the glory of the Lord in the temple (2 Chron. 7:1).

13. The same Spirit of God, which "swept over the face of the waters" in creation, descended on Mary (Luke 1:35) and brought forth Jesus. It was the Holy Spirit who empowered Jesus at his baptism (Mark 1:10) and commissioned him for his mission (Luke 4:14, 18). Jesus Christ, full of the Spirit of God, died on the cross. He gave up the spirit (John 19:30). In death, in the coldness of the tomb, by the power of the Holy Spirit he was raised to life, the firstborn from the dead (Rom. 8:11).

14. After his resurrection, Jesus Christ appeared to his community and sent his disciples in mission: "As the Father has sent me, so I send you" (John 20:21-22). By the gift of the Holy Spirit, "the power from on high," they were formed into a new community of witness to hope in Christ (Luke 24:49; Acts 1:8). In the Spirit of unity, the early church lived together and shared her goods among her members (Acts 2:44-45).

15. The universality of the Spirit's economy in creation and the particularity of the Spirit's work in redemption have to be understood together as the mission of the Spirit for the new heaven and earth, when God finally will be "all in all" (1 Cor. 15:24-28). The Holy Spirit works in the world often in mysterious and unknown ways beyond our imagination (Luke 1:34-35; John 3:8; Acts 2:16-21).

16. Biblical witness attests to a variety of understandings of the role of the Holy Spirit in mission. One perspective on the role of the Holy Spirit in mission emphasizes the Holy Spirit as fully dependent on Christ, as the Paraclete and the one who will come as Counselor and Advocate only after Christ has gone to the Father. The Holy Spirit is seen as the continuing presence of Christ, his agent to fulfill the task of mission. This understanding leads to a missiology focusing on sending out and going forth. Therefore, a pneumatological focus on Christian mission recognizes that mission is essentially

christologically based and relates the work of the Holy Spirit to the salvation through Jesus Christ.

17.   Another perspective emphasizes that the Holy Spirit is the "Spirit of Truth" that leads us to the "whole truth" (John 16:13) and blows wherever he/she wills (John 3:8), thus embracing the whole of the cosmos; it proclaims the Holy Spirit as the source of Christ and the church as the eschatological coming together (*synaxis*) of the people of God in God's kingdom. This second perspective posits that the faithful go forth in peace (in mission) after they have experienced in their eucharistic gathering the eschatological kingdom of God as a glimpse and foretaste of it. Mission as going forth is thus the outcome, rather than the origin of the church, and is called "liturgy after the Liturgy."[3]

18.   What is clear is that by the Spirit we participate in the mission of love that is at the heart of the life of the Trinity. This results in Christian witness which unceasingly proclaims the salvific power of God through Jesus Christ and constantly affirms God's dynamic involvement, through the Holy Spirit, in the whole created world. All who respond to the outpouring of the love of God are invited to join in with the Spirit in the mission of God.

Mission and the Flourishing of Creation

19.   Mission is the overflow of the infinite love of the Triune God. God's mission begins with the act of creation. Creation's life and God's life are entwined. The mission of God's Spirit encompasses us all in an ever-giving act of grace. We are therefore called to move beyond a narrowly human-centred approach and to embrace forms of mission which express our reconciled relationship with all created life. We hear the cry of the earth as we listen to the cries of the poor and we know that from its beginning the earth has cried out to God over humanity's injustice (Gen. 4:10).

---

3. See Ion Bria, *The Liturgy after the Liturgy: Mission and Witness from an Orthodox Perspective* (Geneva: WCC Publications, 1996). The term was originally coined by Archbishop Anastasios Yannoulatos and widely publicized by Ion Bria.

20.   Mission with creation at its heart is already a positive movement in our churches through campaigns for eco-justice and more sustainable lifestyles and the development of spiritualities that are respectful of the earth. However, we have sometimes forgotten that the whole of creation is included in the reconciled unity towards which we are all called (2 Cor. 5:18-19). We do not believe that the earth is to be discarded and only souls saved; both the earth and our bodies have to be transformed through the Spirit's grace. As the vision of Isaiah and John's revelation testify, heaven and earth will be made new (Is. 11:1-9; 25:6-10; 66:22; Rev. 21:1-4).

21.   Our participation in mission, our being in creation, and our practice of the life of the Spirit need to be woven together, for they are mutually transformative. We ought not to seek the one without the others. If we do, we will lapse into an individualistic spirituality that leads us to believe falsely that we can belong to God without belonging to our neighbour, and we will fall into a spirituality that simply makes us feel good while other parts of creation hurt and yearn.

22.   We need a new conversion (*metanoia*) in our mission which invites a new humility in regard to the mission of God's Spirit. We tend to understand and practice mission as something done by humanity *to* others. Instead, humans can participate in communion *with* all of creation in celebrating the work of the Creator. In many ways creation is in mission to humanity; for instance, the natural world has a power that can heal the human heart and body. The wisdom literature in the Bible affirms creation's praise of its Creator (Ps. 9:1-4; 66:1; 96:11-13; 98:4; 100:1; 150:6). The Creator's joy and wonder in creation is one of the sources of our spirituality (Job 38–39).

23.   We want to affirm our spiritual connection with creation, yet the reality is that the earth is being polluted and exploited. Consumerism triggers not limitless growth but rather endless exploitation of the earth's resources. Human greed is contributing to global warming and other forms of climate change. If this trend continues

and earth is fatally damaged, what can we imagine salvation to be? Humanity cannot be saved alone while the rest of the created world perishes. Eco-justice cannot be separated from salvation, and salvation cannot come without a new humility that respects the needs of all life on earth.

Spiritual Gifts and Discernment

24. The Holy Spirit gives gifts freely and impartially (1 Cor. 12:8-10; Rom. 12:6-8; Eph. 4:11) which are to be shared for the building up of others (1 Cor. 12:7; 14:26) and the reconciliation of the whole creation (Rom. 8:19-23). One of the gifts of the Spirit is discernment of spirits (1 Cor. 12:10). We discern the Spirit of God wherever life in its fullness is affirmed and in all its dimensions, including liberation of the oppressed, healing and reconciliation of broken communities, and the restoration of creation. We also discern evil spirits wherever forces of death and destruction of life prevail.

25. The early Christians, like many today, experienced a world of many spirits. The New Testament witnesses to diverse spirits, including evil spirits, "ministering spirits" (i.e. angels, Heb. 1:14), "principalities" and "powers" (Eph. 6:12), the beast (Rev. 13:1-7), and other powers—both good and evil. The apostle Paul also testifies to some spiritual struggle (Eph. 6:10-18; 2 Cor. 10:4-6) and other apostolic writings contain injunctions to resist the devil (James 4:7; 1 Pet. 5:8). The churches are called to discern the work of the life-giving Spirit sent into the world and to join with the Holy Spirit in bringing about God's reign of justice (Acts 1:6-8). When we have discerned the Holy Spirit's presence, we are called to respond, recognizing that God's Spirit is often subversive, leading us beyond boundaries and surprising us.

26. Our encounter with the Triune God is inward, personal, and communal but also directs us outward in missionary endeavour. The traditional symbols and titles for the Spirit (such as fire, light, dew, fountain, anointing, healing, melting, warming, solace, comfort,

strength, rest, washing, shining) show that the Spirit is familiar with our lives and connected with all the aspects of relationship, life, and creation with which mission is concerned. We are led by the Spirit into various situations and moments, into meeting points with others, into spaces of encounter, and into critical locations of human struggle.

27.   The Holy Spirit is the Spirit of wisdom (Is. 11:3; Eph. 1:17) and guides us into all truth (John 16:13). The Spirit inspires human cultures and creativity, so it is part of our mission to acknowledge, respect, and cooperate with life-giving wisdoms in every culture and context. We regret that mission activity linked with colonization has often denigrated cultures and failed to recognize the wisdom of local people. Local wisdom and culture which are life-affirming are gifts from God's Spirit. We lift up testimonies of peoples whose traditions have been scorned and mocked by theologians and scientists, yet whose wisdom offers us the vital and sometimes new orientation that can connect us again with the life of the Spirit in creation, which helps us to consider the ways in which God is revealed in creation.

28.   The claim that the Spirit is with us is not for us to make, but for others to recognize in the life that we lead. The apostle Paul expresses this by encouraging the church to bear the fruits of the Spirit which entail love, joy, peace, patience, kindness, generosity, faithfulness, and self-control (Gal. 5:23). As we bear these fruits, we hope others will discern the love and power of the Spirit at work.

Transformative Spirituality

29.   Authentic Christian witness is not only in *what* we do in mission but *how* we live out our mission. The church in mission can only be sustained by spiritualities deeply rooted in the Trinity's communion of love. Spirituality gives our lives their deepest meaning. It stimulates, motivates and gives dynamism to life's journey. It is energy

for life in its fullness and calls for a commitment to resist all forces, powers, and systems which deny, destroy, and reduce life.

30.   Mission spirituality is always transformative. Mission spirituality resists and seeks to transform all life-destroying values and systems wherever these are at work in our economies, our politics, and even our churches. "Our faithfulness to God and God's free gift of life compels us to confront idolatrous assumptions, unjust systems, politics of domination and exploitation in our current world economic order. Economics and economic justice are always matters of faith as they touch the very core of God's will for creation."[4] Mission spirituality motivates us to serve God's economy of life, not mammon, to share life at God's table rather than satisfy individual greed, to pursue change toward a better world while challenging the self-interest of the powerful who desire to maintain the status quo.

31.   Jesus has told us "You cannot serve God and mammon" (Matt. 6:24, KJV). The policy of unlimited growth through the domination of the global free market is an ideology that claims to be without alternative, demanding an endless flow of sacrifices from the poor and from nature. "It makes the false promise that it can save the world through creation of wealth and prosperity, claiming sovereignty over life and demanding total allegiance, which amounts to idolatry."[5] This is a global system of mammon that protects the unlimited growth of wealth of only the rich and powerful through endless exploitation. This tower of greed is threatening the whole household of God. The reign of God is in direct opposition to the empire of mammon.

32.   Transformation can be understood in the light of the Paschal mystery: "If we have died with Christ, we will also live with him; if we endure, we will also reign with him" (2 Tim. 2:11-12). In situations of oppression, discrimination, and hurt, the cross of Christ is the

---

4. *Alternative Globalization Addressing Peoples and Earth (AGAPE): A Background Document* (Geneva: WCC Publications, 2005), 13.
5. World Alliance of Reformed Churches, *The Accra Confession: Covenanting for Justice: in the Economy and the Earth* (2004), §10.

power of God for salvation (1 Cor. 1:18). Even in our time, some have paid with their lives for their Christian witness, reminding us all of the cost of discipleship. The Spirit gives Christians courage to live out their convictions, even in the face of persecution and martyrdom.

33.   The cross calls for repentance in light of misuse of power and use of the wrong kind of power in mission and in the church. "Disturbed by the asymmetries and imbalances of power that divide and trouble us in church and world, we are called to repentance, to critical reflection on systems of power, and to accountable use of power structures."[6] The Spirit empowers the powerless and challenges the powerful to empty themselves of their privileges for the sake of the disempowered.

34.   To experience life in the Spirit is to taste life in its fullness. We are called to witness to a movement toward life, celebrating all that the Spirit continues to call into being, walking in solidarity in order to cross the rivers of despair and anxiety (Ps. 23, Is. 43:1-5). Mission provokes in us a renewed awareness that the Holy Spirit meets us and challenges us at all levels of life and brings newness and change to the places and times of our personal and collective journeys.

35.   The Holy Spirit is present with us as companion, yet is never domesticated or "tame." Among the surprises of the Spirit are the ways in which God works from locations which appear to be on the margins and through people who appear to be excluded.

Spirit of Liberation: Mission from the Margins

36.   God's purpose for the world is not to create another world, but to re-create what God has already created in love and wisdom. Jesus began his ministry by claiming that to be filled by the Spirit is to

---

6. Edinburgh 2010, *Common Call* (2010), § 4.

liberate the oppressed, to open eyes that are blind, and to announce the coming of God's reign (Luke 4:16-18). He went about fulfilling this mission by opting to be with the marginalized people of his time, not out of paternalistic charity but because their situations testified to the sinfulness of the world and their yearnings for life pointed to God's purposes.

37.   Jesus Christ relates to and embraces those who are most marginalized in society, in order to confront and transform all that denies life. This includes cultures and systems which generate and sustain massive poverty, discrimination, and dehumanization, and which exploit or destroy people and the earth. Mission from the margins calls for an understanding of the complexities of power dynamics, global systems and structures, and local contextual realities. Christian mission has at times been understood and practiced in ways which failed to recognize God's alignment with those consistently pushed to the margins. Therefore, mission from the margins invites the church to re-imagine mission as a vocation from God's Spirit who works for a world where the fullness of life is available for all.

Why Margins and Marginalization?

38.   Mission from the margins seeks to counteract injustices in life, church, and mission. It seeks to be an alternative missional movement against the perception that mission can only be done by the powerful to the powerless, by the rich to the poor, or by the privileged to the marginalized. Such approaches can contribute to oppression and marginalization. Mission from the margins recognizes that being in the centre means having access to systems that lead to one's rights, freedom, and individuality being affirmed and respected; living in the margins means exclusion from justice and dignity. Living on the margins, however, can provide its own lessons. People on the margins have agency, and can often see what, from the centre, is out of view. People on the margins, living in vulnerable positions, often know what exclusionary forces are threatening their survival and can best discern the urgency of their struggles; people in positions

of privilege have much to learn from the daily struggles of people living in marginal conditions.

39. Marginalized people have God-given gifts that are under-utilized because of disempowerment and denial of access to opportunities and/or justice. Through struggles in and for life, marginalized people are reservoirs of the active hope, collective resistance, and perseverance that are needed to remain faithful to the promised reign of God.

40. Because the context of missional activity influences its scope and character, the social location of all engaged in mission work must be taken into account. Missiological reflections need to recognize the different value orientations that shape missional perspectives. The aim of mission is not simply to move people from the margins to centres of power but to confront those who remain the centre by keeping people on the margins. Instead, churches are called to *transform* power structures.

41. The dominant expressions of mission, in the past and today, have often been directed *at* people on the margins of societies. These have generally viewed those on the margins as recipients and not as active agents of missionary activity. Mission expressed in this way has too often been complicit with oppressive and life-denying systems. It has generally aligned with the privileges of the centre and largely failed to challenge economic, social, cultural, and political systems which have marginalized some peoples. Mission from the centre is motivated by an attitude of paternalism and a superiority complex. Historically, this stance has equated Christianity with Western culture and resulted in adverse consequences, including the denial of the full personhood of the victims of such marginalization.

42. A major common concern of people from the margins is the failure of societies, cultures, civilizations, nations, and even churches to honour the dignity and worth of *all* persons. Injustice is at the

roots of the inequalities that give rise to marginalization and oppression. God's desire for justice is inextricably linked to God's nature and sovereignty: "For the Lord your God is God of gods and Lord of lords ... who executes justice for the orphan and the widow, and who also loves the strangers, providing them food and clothing" (Deut. 10:17-18). All missional activity must, therefore, safeguard the sacred worth of every human being and of the earth (see Is. 58).

Mission as Struggle and Resistance

43.   The affirmation of God's mission (*missio Dei*) points to the belief in God as One who acts in history and in creation, in concrete realities of time and contexts, who seeks the fullness of life for the whole earth through justice, peace, and reconciliation. Participation in God's ongoing work of liberation and reconciliation by the Holy Spirit, therefore, includes discerning and unmasking the demons that exploit and enslave. For example, this involves deconstructing patriarchal ideologies, upholding the right to self-determination for Indigenous peoples, and challenging the social embeddedness of racism and casteism.

44.   The church's hope is rooted in the promised fulfillment of the reign of God. It entails the restoration of right relationships between God and humanity and all of creation. Even though this vision speaks to an eschatological reality, it deeply energizes and informs our current participation in God's salvific work in this penultimate period.

45.   Participation in God's mission follows the way of Jesus, who came to serve, not to be served (Mark 10:45); who tears down the mighty and powerful and exalts the lowly (Luke 1:46-55); and whose love is characterized by mutuality, reciprocity, and interdependence. It therefore requires a commitment to struggle against and resist the powers that obstruct the fullness of life that God wills for all, and a willingness to work with all people involved in movements and initiatives committed to the causes of justice, dignity, and life.

Mission Seeking Justice and Inclusivity

46. The good news of God's reign is about the promise of the actual-ization of a just and inclusive world. Inclusivity fosters just rela-tionships in the community of humanity and creation, with mutual acknowledgement of persons and creation and mutual respect and sustenance of each one's sacred worth. It also facilitates each one's full participation in the life of the community. Baptism in Christ implies a lifelong commitment to give an account of this hope by overcoming the barriers in order to find a common identity under the sovereignty of God (Gal. 3:27-28). Therefore, discrimination of all types against any human beings is unacceptable in the sight of God.

47. Jesus promises that the last shall be first (Matt. 20:16). To the extent that the church practices radical hospitality to the estranged in society, it demonstrates commitment to embodying the values of the reign of God (Is. 58:6). To the extent that it denounces self-centredness as a way of life, it makes space for the reign of God to permeate human existence. To the extent that it renounces violence in its physical, psychological, and spiritual manifestations both in personal interactions and in economic, political, and social systems, it testifies to the reign of God at work in the world.

48. In reality, however, mission, money, and political power are strate-gic partners. Although our theological and missiological language talks a lot about the mission of the church being in solidarity with the poor, sometimes in practice it is much more concerned with being in the centres of power, eating with the rich, and lobbying for money to maintain ecclesial bureaucracy. This poses particular challenges to reflect on what is the good news for people who are privileged and powerful.

49. The church is called to make present God's holy and life-affirming plan for the world revealed in Jesus Christ. This means rejecting values and practices which lead to the destruction of community.

Christians are called to acknowledge the sinful nature of all forms of discrimination and to transform unjust structures. This call places certain expectations on the church. The church must refuse to harbour oppressive forces within its ranks, acting instead as a counter-cultural community. The biblical mandate to the covenant community in both testaments is characterized by the dictum "It shall not be so among you" (Matt. 20:26, KJV).

Mission as Healing and Wholeness

50.   Actions towards healing and wholeness of life of persons and communities are an important expression of mission. Healing was not only a central feature of Jesus' ministry but also a feature of his call to his followers to continue his work (Matt. 10:1). Healing is also one of the gifts of the Holy Spirit (1 Cor. 12:9; Acts 3). The Spirit empowers the church for a life-nurturing mission, which includes prayer, pastoral care, and professional health care on the one hand and prophetic denunciation of the root causes of suffering, transformation of structures that dispense injustice, and pursuit of scientific research on the other.

51.   Health is more than physical and/or mental well-being and healing is not primarily medical. This understanding of health coheres with the biblical-theological tradition of the church, which sees a human being as a multidimensional unity and the body, soul, and mind as interrelated and interdependent. It thus affirms the social, political, and ecological dimensions of personhood and wholeness. Health, in the sense of wholeness, is a condition related to God's promise for the end of time as well as a real possibility in the present.[7] Wholeness is not a static balance of harmony but rather involves living-in-community with God, people, and creation. Individualism and injustice are barriers to community building and therefore to wholeness. Discrimination on grounds of medical conditions or disability—including HIV and AIDS—is contrary to the teaching of Jesus Christ. When all the parts of our individual and corporate

7. *Healing and Wholeness: The Churches' Role in Health* (Geneva: WCC Publications, 1990), 6.

lives that have been left out are included, and wherever the neglected or marginalized are brought together in love such that wholeness is experienced, we may discern signs of God's reign on earth.

52.   Societies have tended to see disability or illness as a manifestation of sin or a medical problem to be solved. The medical model has emphasized the correction or cure of what is assumed to be the "deficiency" in the individual. Many who are marginalized, however, do not see themselves as "deficient" or "sick." The Bible recounts many instances where Jesus healed people with various infirmities but, equally importantly, he restored people to their rightful places within the fabric of the community. Healing is more about the restoration of wholeness than about correcting something perceived as defective. To become whole, the parts that have become estranged need to be reclaimed. The fixation on cure is thus a perspective that must be overcome in order to promote the biblical focus. Mission should foster the full participation of people with disabilities and illness in the life of the church and society.

53.   Christian medical mission aims at achieving health for all in the sense that all people around the globe will have access to quality health care. There are many ways in which churches can be, and are, involved in health and healing in a comprehensive sense. They create or support clinics and mission hospitals; they offer counseling services, care groups, and health programmes; local churches can create groups to visit sick congregation members. Healing processes could include praying with and for the sick, confession and forgiveness, the laying on of hands, anointing with oil, and the use of charismatic spiritual gifts (1 Cor. 12). But it must also be noted that inappropriate forms of Christian worship, including triumphalistic healing services in which the healer is glorified at the expense of God and false expectations are raised, can deeply harm people. This is not to deny God's miraculous intervention of healing in some cases.

54. As a community of imperfect people, and as part of a creation groaning in pain and longing for its liberation, the Christian community can be a sign of hope and an expression of the kingdom of God here on earth (Rom. 8:22-24). The Holy Spirit works for justice and healing in many ways and is pleased to indwell the particular community which is called to embody Christ's mission.

Spirit of Community: Church on the Move

God's Mission and the Life of the Church

55. The life of the church arises from the love of the Triune God. "God is love" (1 Jn. 4:8). Mission is a response to God's urging love shown in creation and redemption. "God's love invites us" (*Caritas Christi urget nos*). This communion (*koinonia*) opens our hearts and lives to our brothers and sisters in the same movement of sharing God's love (2 Cor. 5:18-21). Living in that love of God, the church is called to become good news for all. The Triune God's overflowing sharing of love is the source of all mission and evangelism.

56. God's love, manifest in the Holy Spirit, is an inspirational gift to all humanity "in all times and places"[8] and for all cultures and situations. The powerful presence of the Holy Spirit, revealed in Jesus Christ, the crucified and risen Lord, initiates us into the fullness of life that is God's gift to each one of us. Through Christ in the Holy Spirit, God indwells the church, revealing God's purposes for the world and empowering and enabling its members to participate in the realization of those purposes.

57. The church in history has not always existed but, both theologically and empirically, came into being for the sake of mission. It is not possible to separate church and mission in terms of their origin or purpose. To fulfill God's missionary purpose is the church's aim. The relationship between church and mission is very intimate because the same Spirit of Christ who empowers the church in mission is

---

8. World Council of Churches, Commission on Faith and Order, *Baptism, Eucharist and Ministry*, Faith and Order Paper No. 111 (Geneva: WCC Publications, 1982), §19.

also the life of the church. At the same time as he sent the church into the world, Jesus Christ breathed the Holy Spirit into the church (John 20:19-23). Therefore, the church exists by mission, just as fire exists by burning. If it does not engage in mission, it ceases to be church.

58.   Starting with God's mission leads to an ecclesiological approach "from below." In this perspective it is not the church that has a mission but rather the mission that has a church. Mission is not a project of expanding churches but of the church embodying God's salvation in this world. Out of this follows a dynamic understanding of the apostolicity of the church: apostolicity is not only safeguarding the faith of the church through the ages but also participating in the apostolate. Thus the churches mainly and foremost need to be missionary churches.

God's Mission and the Church's Unity

59.   Living out our faith in community is an important way of participating in mission. Through baptism, we become sisters and brothers belonging together in Christ (Heb. 10:25). The church is called to be an inclusive community that welcomes all. Through word and deed and in its very being, the church foretastes and witnesses to the vision of the coming reign of God. The church is the *coming together* of the faithful and their *going forth* in peace.

60.   Practically as well as theologically, mission and unity belong together. In this regard, the integration in 1961 of the International Missionary Council (IMC) and the World Council of Churches (WCC) was a significant step. This historical experience encourages us to believe that mission and church can come together. This aim, however, is not yet fully accomplished. We have to continue this journey in our century with fresh attempts so that the church becomes truly missionary.

61.   The churches realize today that in many respects they are still not adequate embodiments of God's mission. Sometimes a sense of separation between mission and church still prevails. The lack of full and real unity in mission still harms the authenticity and credibility of the fulfillment of God's mission in this world. Our Lord prayed "that they may all be one ... so that the world may believe" (John 17:21). Thus mission and unity are intertwined. Consequently there is a need to open up our reflections on church and unity to an even wider understanding of unity: the unity of humanity and even the cosmic unity of the whole of God's creation.

62.   The highly competitive environment of the free market economy has unfortunately influenced some churches and para-church movements to seek to be "winners" over others. This can even lead to the adoption of aggressive tactics to persuade Christians who already belong to a church to change their denominational allegiance. Seeking numerical growth at all costs is incompatible with the respect for others required of Christian disciples. Jesus became our Christ not through power or money but through his self-emptying (*kenosis*) and death on the cross. This humble understanding of mission does not merely shape our methods but is the very nature and essence of our faith in Christ. The church is a servant in God's mission and not the master. The missionary church glorifies God in self-emptying love.

63.   The Christian communities in their diversity are called to identify and practice ways of common witness in a spirit of partnership and cooperation, including through mutually respectful and responsible forms of evangelism. Common witness is what the "churches, even while separated, bear together, especially through joint efforts, by manifesting whatever divine gifts of truth and life they already share and experience in common."[9]

---

9. Thomas F. Best and Günther Gassmann, eds., *On the Way to Fuller Koinonia: Official Report of the Fifth World Conference on Faith and Order, Santiago de Compostela 1993*, Faith and Order Paper no. 166 (Geneva: WCC Publications, 1994), 254.

64. The missionary nature of the church also means that there must be a way that churches and para-church structures can be more closely related. The integration of the IMC and the WCC brought about a new framework for consideration of church unity and mission. While discussions of unity have been very concerned with structural questions, mission agencies can represent flexibility and subsidiarity in mission. While para-church movements can find accountability and direction through ecclesial mooring, para-church structures can help churches not to forget their dynamic apostolic character.

65. The Commission on World Mission and Evangelism (CWME), the direct heir of Edinburgh 1910's initiatives on cooperation and unity, provides a structure for churches and mission agencies to seek ways of expressing and strengthening unity in mission. Being an integral part of the WCC, the CWME has been able to encounter new understandings of mission and unity from Catholic, Orthodox, Anglican, Protestant, Evangelical, Pentecostal, and Indigenous churches from all over the globe. In particular, the context of the WCC has facilitated close working relationships with the Roman Catholic Church. A growing intensity of collaboration with Evangelicals, especially with the Lausanne Movement for World Evangelization and the World Evangelical Alliance, has also abundantly contributed to the enrichment of ecumenical theological reflection on mission in unity. Together we share a common concern that the whole church should witness to the whole gospel in the whole world.[10]

66. The Holy Spirit, the Spirit of unity, unites people and churches too, to celebrate unity in diversity both proactively and constructively. The Spirit provides both the dynamic context and the resources needed for people to explore differences in a safe, positive and nurturing environment in order to grow into an inclusive and mutually responsible community.

---

10. See "The Whole Church Taking the Whole Gospel to the Whole World: Reflections of the Lausanne Theology Working Group" (2010).

God Empowers the Church in Mission

67.   Through Christ in the Holy Spirit, God indwells the church, empowering and energizing its members. Thus mission becomes for Christians an urgent inner compulsion (1 Cor. 9:16) and even a test and criterion for authentic life in Christ, rooted in the profound demands of Christ's love, to invite others to share in the fullness of life Jesus came to bring. Participating in God's mission, therefore, should be natural for all Christians and all churches, not only for particular individuals or specialized groups.[11]

68.   What makes the Christian message of God's abundant love for humanity and all creation credible is our ability to speak with one voice, where possible, and to give common witness and an account of the hope that is in us (1 Pet. 3:15). The churches have therefore produced a rich array of common declarations, some of them resulting in uniting or united churches, and of dialogues, seeking to restore the unity of all Christians in one living organism of healing and reconciliation. A rediscovery of the work of the Holy Spirit in healing and reconciliation, which is at the heart of today's mission theology, has significant ecumenical implications.[12]

69.   While acknowledging the great importance of "visible" unity among churches, nonetheless unity need not be sought only at the level of organizational structures. From a mission perspective, it is important to discern what helps the cause of God's mission. In other words, unity in mission is the basis for the visible unity of the churches; this also has implications for the order of the church. Attempts to achieve unity must be in concert with the biblical call to seek justice. Our call to do justice may sometimes involve breaking false unities that silence and oppress. Genuine unity always entails inclusivity and respect for others.

---

11. "Mission and Evangelism in Unity," CWME Study Document (2000), §13.
12. See "Mission as Ministry of Reconciliation," in *You Are the Light of the World: Statements on Mission by the World Council of Churches 1980-2005*, ed. Jacques Matthey (Geneva: WCC Publications, 2005), 90-162.

70. Today's context of large-scale worldwide migration challenges the churches' commitment to unity in very practical ways. We are told: "Do not forget to entertain strangers, for by so doing some people have entertained angels without knowing it." (Heb. 13:2, NIV). Churches can be a place of refuge for migrant communities; they can also be intentional focal points for intercultural engagement.[13] The churches are called to be one to serve God's mission beyond ethnic and cultural boundaries and ought to create multi-cultural ministry and mission as a concrete expression of common witness in diversity. This may entail advocating justice in regard to migration policies and resistance to xenophobia and racism. Women, children, and undocumented workers are often the most vulnerable among migrants in all contexts. But women are also often at the cutting edge of new migrant ministries.

71. God's hospitality calls us to move beyond binary notions of culturally dominant groups as hosts and migrant and minority peoples as guests. Instead, in God's hospitality, God is host and we are all invited by the Spirit to participate with humility and mutuality in God's mission.

Local Congregations: New Initiatives

72. While cherishing the unity of the Spirit in the one Church, it is also important to honour the ways in which each local congregation is led by the Spirit to respond to its own contextual realities. Today's changed world calls for local congregations to take new initiatives. For example, in the secularizing global North, new forms of contextual mission such as "new monasticism," "emerging church," and "fresh expressions," have redefined and revitalized churches. Exploring contextual ways of being church can be particularly relevant to young people. Some churches in the global North now meet in pubs, coffee houses, or converted movie theatres. Engaging with

---

13. "Report of WCC Consultation on Mission and Ecclesiology of the Migrant Churches, Utrecht, the Netherlands, 16-21 November 2010," *International Review of Mission*, 100.1 392 (April 2011): 104-107.

church life online is an attractive option for young people thinking in a non-linear, visual, and experiential way.

73.   Like the early church in the Book of Acts, local congregations have the privilege of forming a community marked by the presence of the risen Christ. For many people, acceptance or refusal to become members of the church is linked to their positive or negative experience with a local congregation, which can be either a stumbling block or an agent of transformation.[14] Therefore it is vital that local congregations are constantly renewed and inspired by the Spirit of mission. Local congregations are frontiers and primary agents of mission.

74.   Worship and the sacraments play a crucial role in the formation of transformative spirituality and mission. Reading the Bible contextually is also a primary resource in enabling local congregations to be messengers and witnesses to God's justice and love. Liturgy in the sanctuary only has full integrity when we live out God's mission in our communities in our daily life. Local congregations are therefore impelled to step out of their comfort zones and cross boundaries for the sake of the mission of God.

75.   More than ever before, local congregations today can play a key role in emphasizing the crossing of cultural and racial boundaries and affirming cultural difference as a gift of the Spirit. Rather than being perceived as a problem, migration can be seen as offering new possibilities for churches to re-discover themselves afresh. It inspires opportunities for the creation of intercultural and multicultural churches at local level. All churches can create space for different cultural communities to come together and embrace exciting opportunities for contextual expressions of intercultural mission in our time.

---

14. Christopher Duraisingh, ed., *Called to One Hope: The Gospel in Diverse Cultures* (Geneva: WCC Publications, 1998), 54.

76. Local congregations can also, as never before, develop global con-
     nections. Many inspirational and transformative linkages are being
     formed between churches that are geographically far apart and
     located in very different contexts. These offer innovative possibili-
     ties but are not without pitfalls. The increasingly popular short-term
     "mission trips" can help to build partnerships between churches in
     different parts of the world but in some cases place an intolerable
     burden on poor local churches or disregard the existing churches
     altogether. While there is some danger and caution around such
     trips, these exposure opportunities in diverse cultural and socio-eco-
     nomic contexts can also lead to long-term change when the travelers
     return to their home community. The challenge is to find ways of
     exercising spiritual gifts which build up the whole church in every
     part (1 Cor. 12-14).

77. Advocacy for justice is no longer the sole prerogative of national
     assemblies and central offices but a form of witness which calls for
     the engagement of local churches. For example, the WCC Decade
     to Overcome Violence (2001-2011) concluded with a plea in the
     International Ecumenical Peace Convocation that "churches must
     help in identifying the everyday choices that can abuse and promote
     human rights, gender justice, climate justice, unity and peace."[15]
     Local churches' grounding in everyday life gives them both legiti-
     macy and motivation in the struggle for justice and peace.

78. The church in every geo-political and socio-economic context is
     called to service (*diakonia*)—to live out the faith and hope of the
     community of God's people, witnessing to what God has done in
     Jesus Christ. Through service the church participates in God's mis-
     sion, following the way of its Servant Lord. The church is called
     to be a diaconal community manifesting the power of service over
     the power of domination, enabling and nurturing possibilities for

---

15. "Glory to God and Peace on Earth: The Message of the International Ecumenical Peace
Convocation," WCC, Kingston, Jamaica, 17-25 May 2011, 2.

life, and witnessing to God's transforming grace through acts of service that hold forth the promise of God's reign.[16]

79.   As the church discovers more deeply its identity as a missionary community, its outward-looking character finds expression in evangelism.

Spirit of Pentecost: Good News for All

The Call to Evangelize

80.   Witness (*martyria*) takes concrete form in evangelism—the communication of the whole gospel to the whole of humanity in the whole world.[17] Its goal is the salvation of the world and the glory of the Triune God. Evangelism is mission activity which makes explicit and unambiguous the centrality of the incarnation, suffering, and resurrection of Jesus Christ without setting limits to the saving grace of God. It seeks to share this good news with all who have not yet heard it and invites them to an experience of life in Christ.

81.   "Evangelism is the outflow of hearts that are filled with the love of God for those who do not yet know him."[18] At Pentecost, the disciples could not but declare the mighty works of God (Acts 2:4; 4:20). Evangelism, while not excluding the different dimensions of mission, focuses on explicit and intentional articulation of the gospel, including "the invitation to personal conversion to a new life in Christ and to discipleship."[19] While the Holy Spirit calls some to be evangelists (Eph. 4:11), we all are called to give an account of the hope that is in us (1 Pet. 3:15). Not only individuals but also the whole church together is called to evangelize (Mark 16:15; 1 Pet. 2:9).

---

16. "*Diakonia* in the Twenty First Century: Theological Perspectives," WCC Conference on Theology of *Diakonia* in the 21st Century, Colombo, Sri Lanka, 2-6 June 2012, 2.
17. *Minutes and Reports of the Fourth Meeting of the Central Committee*, WCC, Rolle, Switzerland, 1951, 66.
18. The Lausanne Movement, *The Cape Town Commitment*, 2010, Part I, 7(b).
19. See Congregation for the Doctrine of the Faith, *Doctrinal Note on Some Aspects of Evangelization*, No. 12, 2007, 489-504.

82.   Today's world is marked by excessive assertion of religious identities and persuasions that seem to break and brutalize in the name of God rather than heal and nurture communities. In such a context, it is important to recognize that proselytism is not a legitimate way of practicing evangelism.[20] The Holy Spirit chooses to work in partnership with people's preaching and demonstration of the good news (see Rom. 10:14-15; 2 Cor. 4:2-6), but it is only God's Spirit who creates new life and brings about rebirth (John 3:5-8; 1 Thess. 1:4-6). We acknowledge that evangelism at times has been distorted and lost its credibility because some Christians have forced "conversions" by violent means or the abuse of power. In some contexts, however, accusations of forced conversions are motivated by the desire of dominant groups to keep the marginalized living with oppressed identities and in dehumanizing conditions.

83.   Evangelism is sharing one's faith and conviction with other people and inviting them to discipleship, whether or not they adhere to other religious traditions. Such sharing is to take place with both confidence and humility and as an expression of our professed love for our world. If we claim to love God and to love our fellow human beings but fail to share the good news with them urgently and consistently, we deceive ourselves as to the integrity of our love for either God or people. There is no greater gift we can offer to our fellow human beings than to share and or introduce them to the love, grace, and mercy of God in Christ.

84.   Evangelism leads to repentance, faith, and baptism. Hearing the truth in the face of sin and evil demands a response—positive or negative (John 4:28-29; cf. Mark 10:22). It provokes conversion, involving a change of attitudes, priorities, and goals. It results in salvation of the lost, healing of the sick, and the liberation of the oppressed and the whole creation.

---

20. WCC Central Committee, *Towards Common Witness: A Call to Adopt Responsible Relationships in Mission and to Renounce Proselytism* (1997).

85.   "Evangelism," while not excluding the different dimensions of mission, focuses on explicit and intentional articulation of the gospel, including "the invitation to personal conversion to a new life in Christ and to discipleship."[21] In different churches, there are differing understandings of how the Spirit calls us to evangelize in our contexts. For some, evangelism is primarily about leading people to personal conversion through Jesus Christ; for others, evangelism is about being in solidarity and offering Christian witness through presence with oppressed peoples; others again look on evangelism as one component of God's mission. Different Christian traditions denote aspects of mission and evangelism in different ways; however, we can still affirm that the Spirit calls us all towards an understanding of evangelism which is grounded in the life of the local church where worship (*leiturgia*) is inextricably linked to witness (*martyria*), service (*diakonia*), and fellowship (*koinonia*).

Evangelism in Christ's Way

86.   Evangelism is sharing the good news both in word and action. Evangelizing through verbal proclamation or preaching of the gospel (*kerygma*) is profoundly biblical. However, if our words are not consistent with our actions, our evangelism is inauthentic. The combination of verbal declaration and visible action bears witness to God's revelation in Jesus Christ and of his purposes. Evangelism is closely related to unity: the love for one another is a demonstration of the gospel we proclaim (John 13:34-35) while disunity is an embarrassment to the gospel (1 Cor. 1).

87.   There are historical and contemporary examples of faithful, humble service by Christians, working in their own local contexts, with whom the Spirit has partnered to bring about fullness of life. Also, many Christians who lived and worked as missionaries far away

---

21. It is important to note that not all churches understand evangelism as expressed in the above. The Roman Catholic Church refers to "evangelization" as the *missio ad gentes* [mission to the peoples] directed to those who do not know Christ. In a wider sense, it is used to describe ordinary pastoral work, while the phrase "new evangelization" designates pastoral outreach to those who no longer practise the Christian faith. See Congregation for the Doctrine of the Faith, Doctrinal Note on Some Aspects of Evangelization.

from their own cultural contexts did so with humility, mutuality, and respect; God's Spirit also stirred in those communities to bring about transformation.

88.   Regrettably, sometimes evangelism has been practiced in ways which betray rather than incarnate the gospel. Whenever this occurs, repentance is in order. Mission in Christ's way involves affirming the dignity and rights of others. We are called to serve others as Christ did (cf. Mark 10:45; Matt. 25:45), without exploitation or any form of allurement.[22] In such individualized contexts, it may be possible to confuse evangelism with buying and selling a "product," where *we* decide what aspects Christian life we want to take on. Instead, the Spirit rejects the idea that Jesus' good news for all can be consumed under capitalist terms, and the Spirit calls us to conversion and transformation at a personal level, which leads us to the proclamation of the fullness of life for all.

89.   Authentic evangelism is grounded in humility and respect for all and flourishes in the context of dialogue. It promotes the message of the gospel, of healing and reconciliation, in word and deed. "There is no evangelism without solidarity; there is no Christian solidarity that does not involve sharing the message of God's coming reign."[23] Evangelism, therefore, inspires the building of inter-personal and community relationships. Such authentic relationships are often best nourished in local faith communities and based in local cultural contexts. Christian witness is as much by our presence as by our words. In situations where the public testimony to one's faith is not possible without risking one's life, simply living the gospel may be a powerful alternative.

---

22. World Council of Churches, Pontifical Council for Interreligious Dialogue, and World Evangelical Alliance, *Christian Witness in a Multi-Religious World: Recommendations for Conduct* (2011).

23. The San Antonio Report, 26; CWME, *Mission and Evangelism: An Ecumenical Affirmation* (1982), §34; Duraisingh, *Called to One Hope*, 38.

90. Aware of tensions between people and communities of different religious convictions and varied interpretations of Christian witness, authentic evangelism must always be guided by life-affirming values, as stated in the joint statement on "Christian Witness in a Multi-Religious World: Recommendations for Conduct":

    a. Rejection of all forms of violence, discrimination and repression by religious and secular authority, including the abuse of power—psychological or social.

    b. Affirming the freedom of religion to practice and profess faith without any fear of reprisal and or intimidation. Mutual respect and solidarity which promote justice, peace and the common good of all.

    c. Respect for all people and human cultures, while also discerning the elements in our own cultures, such as patriarchy, racism, casteism, etc., that need to be challenged by the gospel.

    d. Renunciation of false witness and listening in order to understand in mutual respect.

    e. Ensuring freedom for ongoing discernment by persons and communities as part of decision-making.

    f. Building relationships with believers of other faiths or no faith to facilitate deeper mutual understanding, reconciliation and cooperation for the common good.[24]

91. We live in a world strongly influenced by individualism, secularism, and materialism and by other ideologies that challenge the values of the kingdom of God. Although the gospel is ultimately good news for all, it is bad news for the forces which promote falsehood, injustice, and oppression. To that extent, evangelism is also a prophetic vocation which involves speaking truth to power in hope and in love (Acts 26:25; Col. 1:5; Eph. 4:15). The gospel is liberative

---

24. See *Christian Witness in a Multi-Religious World.*

and transformative. Its proclamation must involve transformation of societies with a view to creating just and inclusive communities.

92.   Standing against evil or injustice and being prophetic can sometimes be met with suppression and violence, and thus consequently lead to suffering, persecution, and even death. Authentic evangelism involves being vulnerable, following the example of Christ by carrying the cross and emptying oneself (Phil. 2:5-11). Just as the blood of the martyrs was the seed of the church under Roman persecution, today the pursuit of justice and righteousness makes a powerful witness to Christ. Jesus linked such self-denial with the call to follow him and with eternal salvation (Mark 8:34-38).

Evangelism, Interfaith Dialogue and Christian Presence

93.   In the plurality and complexity of today's world, we encounter people of many different faiths, ideologies, and convictions. We believe that the Spirit of Life brings joy and fullness of life. God's Spirit, therefore, can be found in all cultures that affirm life. The Holy Spirit works in mysterious ways and we do not fully understand the workings of the Spirit in other faith traditions. We acknowledge that there is inherent value and wisdom in diverse life-giving spiritualities. Therefore, authentic mission makes the "other" a partner in, not an "object" of mission.

94.   Dialogue is a way of affirming our common life and goals in terms of the affirmation of life and the integrity of creation. Dialogue at the religious level is possible only if we begin with the expectation of meeting God who has preceded us and has been present with people within their own contexts.[25] God is there before we come (Acts 17) and our task is not to bring God along, but to witness to the God who is already there. Dialogue provides for an honest encounter where each party brings to the table all that they are in an open, patient and respectful manner.

---

25. See WCC, *Baar Statement: Theological Perspectives on Plurality* (1990).

95. Evangelism and dialogue are distinct but interrelated. Although Christians hope and pray that all people may come to living knowledge of the Triune God, evangelism is not the purpose of dialogue. However, since dialogue is also "a mutual encounter of commitments," sharing the good news of Jesus Christ has a legitimate place in it. Furthermore, authentic evangelism takes place in the context of the dialogue of life and action and in "the spirit of dialogue"— "an attitude of respect and friendship."[26] Evangelism entails not only proclamation of our deepest convictions, but also listening to others and being challenged and enriched by others (Acts 10).

96. Particularly important is dialogue between people of different faiths, not only in multi-religious contexts but equally where there is a large majority of a particular faith. It is necessary to protect rights of minority groups and religious freedom and to enable all to contribute to the common good. Religious freedom should be upheld because it flows from the dignity of the human person, grounded in the creation of all human beings in the image and likeness of God (Gen. 1:26). Followers of all religions and beliefs have equal rights and responsibilities.[27]

Evangelism and Cultures

97. The gospel takes root in different contexts through engagement with specific cultural, political, and religious realities. Respect for people and their cultural and symbolic life-worlds are necessary if the gospel is to take root in those different realities. In this way it must begin with engagement and dialogue with the wider context in order to discern how Christ is already present and where God's Spirit is already at work.

98. The connection of evangelism with colonial powers in the history of mission has led to the presupposition that Western forms

---

26. Pontifical Council for Inter-Religious Dialogue, *Dialogue and Proclamation: Reflection and Orientations on Interreligious Dialogue and the Proclamation of The Gospel of Jesus Christ* (1991), §9.
27. See *Christian Witness in a Multi-Religious World.*

of Christianity are the standards by which others' adherence to the gospel should be judged. Evangelism by those who enjoy economic power or cultural hegemony risks distorting the gospel. Therefore, they must seek the partnership of the poor, the dispossessed, and minorities and be shaped by their theological resources and visions.

99.   The enforcement of uniformity discredits the uniqueness of each individual created in the image and likeness of God. Whereas Babel attempted to enforce uniformity, the preaching of the disciples on the day of Pentecost resulted in a unity in which personal particularities and community identities were not lost but respected—they heard the good news in their own languages.

100.   Jesus calls us out of the narrow concerns of *our* own kingdom, *our* own liberation, and *our* own independence (Acts 1:6) by unveiling to us a larger vision and empowering us by the Holy Spirit to go "to the ends of the earth" as witnesses in each context of time and space to God's justice, freedom, and peace. Our calling is to point all to Jesus, rather than to ourselves or our institutions, looking out for the interests of others rather than our own (see Phil. 2:3-4). We cannot capture the complexities of the scriptures through one dominant cultural perspective. A plurality of cultures is a gift of the Spirit to deepen our understanding of our faith and one another. As such, intercultural communities of faith, where diverse cultural communities worship together, is one way in which cultures can engage one another authentically and where culture can enrich gospel. At the same time, the gospel critiques notions of cultural superiority. Therefore, "the gospel, to be fruitful, needs to be both true to itself and incarnated or rooted in the culture of a people ... We need constantly to seek the insight of the Holy Spirit in helping us to better discern where the gospel challenges, endorses or transforms a particular culture"[28] for the sake of life.

---

28. *Called to One Hope*, 21-22; 24.

Feast of Life: Concluding Affirmations

101. We are the servants of the Triune God, who has given us the mission of proclaiming the good news to all humanity and creation,
especially the oppressed and the suffering people who are longing
for fullness of life. Mission—as a common witness to Christ—is
an invitation to the "feast in the kingdom of God" (Luke 14:15).
The mission of the church is to prepare the banquet and to invite
all people to the feast of life. The feast is a celebration of creation
and fruitfulness overflowing from the love of God, the source of
life in abundance. It is a sign of the liberation and reconciliation
of the whole creation which is the goal of mission. With a renewed
appreciation of the mission of God's Spirit, we offer the following
affirmations in response to the question posed at the beginning of
this document.

102. *We affirm that the purpose of God's mission is fullness of life (John
10:10) and that this is the criterion for discernment in mission.* Therefore, we are called to discern the Spirit of God wherever there is life
in its fullness, particularly in terms of the liberation of the oppressed
peoples, the healing and reconciliation of broken communities, and
the restoration of the whole creation. We are challenged to appreciate the life-affirming spirits present in different cultures and to be in
solidarity with all those who are involved in the mission of affirming
and preserving life. We also discern and confront evil spirits wherever forces of death and negation of life are experienced.

103. *We affirm that mission begins with God's act of creation and continues
in re-creation, by the enlivening power of the Holy Spirit.* The Holy
Spirit, poured out in tongues of fire at Pentecost, fills our hearts
and makes us into Christ's church. The Spirit which was in Christ
Jesus inspires us to a self-emptying and cross-bearing life-style and
accompanies God's people as we seek to bear witness to the love of
God in word and deed. The Spirit of truth leads into all truth and
empowers us to defy the demonic powers and speak the truth in

love. As a redeemed community we share with others the waters of life and look for the Spirit of unity to heal, reconcile, and renew the whole creation.

104. *We affirm that spirituality is the source of energy for mission and that mission in the Spirit is transformative.* Thus we seek a re-orienting of our perspective between mission, spirituality, and creation. Mission spirituality that flows from liturgy and worship reconnects us with one another and with the wider creation. We understand that our participation in mission, our existence in creation, and our practice of the life of the Spirit are woven together, for they are mutually transformative. Mission that begins with creation invites us to celebrate life in all its dimensions as God's gift.

105. *We affirm that the mission of God's Spirit is to renew the whole creation.* "The earth is the Lord's and everything in it" (Ps. 24:1, NIV). The God of life protects, loves, and cares for nature. Humanity is not the master of the earth but is responsible to care for the integrity of creation. Excessive greed and unlimited consumption which lead to continuous destruction of nature must end. God's love does not proclaim a human salvation separate from the renewal of the whole creation. We are called to participate in God's mission beyond our human-centred goals. God's mission is to all life and we have to both acknowledge it and serve it in new ways of mission. We pray for repentance and forgiveness, but we also call for action now. Mission has creation at its heart.

106. *We affirm that today mission movements are emerging from the global South and East which are multi-directional and many-faceted.* The shifting centre of gravity of Christianity to the global South and East challenges us to explore missiological expressions that are rooted in these contexts, culture, and spiritualities. We need to develop further mutuality and partnership and affirm interdependence within mission and the ecumenical movement. Our mission practice should show solidarity with suffering peoples and harmony with nature.

Evangelism is done in self-emptying humility, with respect towards others and in dialogue with people of different cultures and faiths. It should, in this landscape, also involve confronting structures and cultures of oppression and dehumanization that are in contradiction to the values of God's reign.

107. *We affirm that marginalized people are agents of mission and exercise a prophetic role which emphasizes that fullness of life is for all.* The marginalized in society are the main partners in God's mission. Marginalized, oppressed, and suffering people have a special gift to distinguish what news is good for them and what news is bad for their endangered life. In order to commit ourselves to God's life-giving mission, we have to listen to the voices from the margins to hear what is life-affirming and what is life-destroying. We must turn our direction of mission to the actions that the marginalized are taking. Justice, solidarity, and inclusivity are key expressions of mission from the margins.

108. *We affirm that the economy of God is based on values of love and justice for all and that transformative mission resists idolatry in the free-market economy.* Economic globalization has effectively supplanted the God of Life with mammon, the god of free-market capitalism that claims the power to save the world through the accumulation of undue wealth and prosperity. Mission in this context needs to be counter-cultural, offering alternatives to such idolatrous visions because mission belongs to the God of Life, justice, and peace and not to this false god who brings misery and suffering to people and nature. Mission, then, is to denounce the economy of greed and to participate in and practice the divine economy of love, sharing, and justice.

109. *We affirm that the gospel of Jesus Christ is good news in all ages and places and should be proclaimed in the Spirit of love and humility.* We affirm the centrality of the incarnation, the cross, and the resurrection in our message and also in the way we do evangelism. Therefore, evangelism always points to Jesus and the kingdom of God rather than to institutions and it belongs to the very being of the

church. The prophetic voice of the church should not be silent in times that demand this voice be heard. The church is called to renew its methods of evangelism to communicate the good news with persuasion, inspiration, and conviction.

110. *We affirm that dialogue and cooperation for life are integral to mission and evangelism.* Authentic evangelism is done with respect for freedom of religion and belief, for all human beings as images of God. Proselytism by violent means, economic incentive, or abuse of power is contrary to the message of the gospel. In doing evangelism it is important to build relations of respect and trust between people of different faiths. We value each and every human culture and recognize that the gospel is not possessed by any group but is for every people. We understand that our task is not to bring God along but to witness to the God who is already there (Acts 17:23-28). Joining in with the Spirit, we are enabled to cross cultural and religious barriers to work together towards life.

111. *We affirm that God moves and empowers the church in mission.* The church as the people of God, the body of Christ, and the temple of the Holy Spirit is dynamic and changing as it continues the mission of God. This leads to a variety of forms of common witness, reflecting the diversity of world Christianity. Thus the churches need to be on the move, journeying together in mission, continuing in the mission of the apostles. Practically, this means that church and mission should be united and that different ecclesial and missional bodies need to work together for the sake of life.

112. The Triune God invites the whole creation to the Feast of Life, through Jesus Christ who came "that they may have life, and may have it in all its fullness" (John 10:10, REB), through the Holy Spirit who affirms the vision of the reign of God, "Behold, I create new heavens and a new earth!" (Is. 65:17, KJV). We commit ourselves together in humility and hope to the mission of God, who recreates all and reconciles all. And we pray, "God of Life, lead us into justice and peace!"

Together towards Life:
A Practical Guide

A Practical Guide

Introduction

What do the terms "mission" and "evangelism" conjure up in your mind? Perhaps a variety of thoughts, some negative and some positive. The 2012 WCC mission affirmation invites us to think of mission, and its implications for evangelism, as the action of the Spirit of God in the life of our world. It traces the origin of mission back to the triune life of God and the love, revealed in Jesus Christ, which God has for humanity and for all creation. The Holy Spirit is the life-giver who sustains and empowers life and renews the whole creation.

The changing landscape of church and mission provides an opportunity for fresh thinking and new forms of action. Gone are the days when Christianity was numerically centred in Europe and North America and mission was understood as taking the gospel to unreached continents. With a growing majority of the world's Christians originating from Asia, Africa and South America, it is time to think of the meaning and direction of mission in new and relevant ways. At a time of change we rediscover that mission is not primarily a human enterprise but a movement that arises from the love of God.

When we receive the Holy Spirit we become part of the mission of God to the life of the world (John 20:22-23). This practical guide to the new mission affirmation offers signposts which can help us to discern the action of the Spirit in the world – and to join in!

The guide provides the opportunity for you to:

- Engage in Bible study which sheds light on the mission affirmation;
- Ponder key points which are made by the mission affirmation;
- Consider stories which provoke thought about contemporary realities;
- Join in prayers inspired by the new mission affirmation;
- Sing songs which resonate with the new mission affirmation;
- Celebrate, reflect and act on your experience with the new mission affirmation.

All of these are intended to be suggestive rather than prescriptive, the appetizer rather than the main course. You are invited to take this text as a springboard which will allow you to identify the biblical texts, the stories and songs and prayers which will embody the thrust of *Together towards Life* in your particular context.

The Spirit of God is at work in the world in ways that bring life and hope. By the gift of the Spirit the disciples of Jesus were formed into a new community of witness to the hope born with his resurrection from the dead. To belong to Jesus today is to be sent on mission, joining in with what the Holy Spirit is doing in the life of the world. This is your invitation to take part.

As well as bringing challenge at a personal level, *Together towards Life* is also intended to give direction to the shaping of future missional work at ecclesial and institutional levels. Churches and church-related agencies for mission and development are invited to evaluate and rethink their mission policy in the light of the ecumenical affirmations of *Together towards Life*. Then they can implement new directions that reflect the changed landscapes.

The new mission affirmation also has significant implications for education and formation. Many church communities look in vain for leaders who enable them to move forward in the power of the Spirit, offering fullness of life for all. *Together towards Life* provides resources to meet this crisis of leadership. It suggests a new approach to leadership formation that involves all members of the faith community employing their unique spiritual gifts to discern and address the critical missionary challenges facing us today.

This action-oriented guide follows the four main divisions of the new mission affirmation:

1. Spirit of Mission: Breath of Life
2. Spirit of Liberation: Mission from the Margins
3. Spirit of Community: Church on the Move
4. Spirit of Pentecost: Good News for All

Each of the four concludes with an invitation to celebrate, reflect and act in regard to three different though inter-related spheres:

- action at local level;
- action in terms of policymaking; and
- action in terms of education and formation.

You are invited to concentrate on the sphere most relevant to your own situation or to draw on all three to develop your own response to *Together towards Life*.

1. Spirit of Mission: Breath of Life

When we look for energy with which to engage in mission, the Bible points us to the empowerment of the Holy Spirit. It is through receiving the Holy Spirit that we are commissioned and sent to play our part in the mission of God. The Holy Spirit leads us into risky places, calls us to build bridges, and invites us to embark on journeys of transformation.

Bible Study: Luke 4:16-30

Luke's Gospel closely links the life and mission of Jesus to the presence and action of the Holy Spirit: annunciation, baptism, temptation in the desert and preaching. In this text, Jesus himself says that the Spirit of God had anointed him for a mission to bring the good news to the afflicted, captives, blind and oppressed.

The Old Testament scriptures introduce us to the Spirit of God who moved over the waters at the beginning, the source of life and the breath of humankind (Genesis 2:7). It is this same Spirit of God who descended on Mary and brought forth Jesus. Now he gives expression to his commissioning by the Spirit and the kind of mission he is called to fulfill.

In the customary way, Jesus read in the synagogue texts from Isaiah 61:1-2 and Isaiah 58:6. These scriptures speak powerfully of good news to the poor, liberty to the captives, recovery of sight to the blind, freedom for the oppressed, and the proclamation of the year of the Lord's favour. Jesus now identifies himself with turning this text into reality.

His mission is a matter of transformation. Life-destroying values and systems will be overcome as the Spirit brings life in all its fullness. Freedom for humanity is allied with renewal of the natural world and justice in the economy. The "year of the Lord's favour" points to the sabbatical year when the land lay fallow and was renewed, and to the jubilee year when debts were cancelled so that the economy would be just and equitable.

The initial response to Jesus' proclamation was positive. Perhaps it was spurred by hopes that Nazareth would have its own pet hero and wonder-worker. Soon, however, the acclamation gave way to furious hostility, especially when Jesus spoke of God's favour to non-Jews, the widow of Zarephath and Naaman the Syrian. If this is what Jesus was about he must be destroyed forthwith! Nazareth is a town surrounded by cliffs and the attempt was made to throw Jesus over one of them. He narrowly escaped with his life.

Questions

1. What did the empowerment of the Spirit mean for the ministry of Jesus? What will it mean for us, in our world, to be empowered by the same Spirit?

2. What situations of poverty, oppression and blindness in your context call for the transformation which God's Spirit brings?

3. What would a "year of the Lord's favour" mean for the renewal and flourishing of the earth today?

4. In a world of many spirits how may we discern the presence and action of the Spirit of God? What clues can we take from Luke 4?

5. Jesus risked his life with his challenge to exclusiveness and vested interests. What risks might we have to take to challenge destructive forces and be part of the transformation which God's Spirit brings to our world?

Food for Thought from Together towards Life

"By the Spirit we participate in the mission of love that is at the heart of the life of the Trinity. This results in Christian witness which unceasingly proclaims the salvific power of God through Jesus Christ and constantly affirms God's dynamic involvement, through the Holy Spirit, in the whole created world. All who respond to the outpouring of the love of God are invited to join in with the Spirit in the mission of God." (TTL-18)

"Consumerism triggers not limitless growth but rather endless exploitation of the earth's resources. Human greed is contributing to global warming and other forms of climate change. If this trend continues and earth is fatally damaged, what can we imagine salvation to be? Humanity cannot be saved alone while the rest of the earth perishes. Eco-justice cannot be separated from salvation, and salvation cannot come without a new humility that respects the needs of all life on earth." (TTL-23)

"When we have discerned the Holy Spirit's presence, we are called to respond, recognizing that God's Spirit is often subversive, leading us beyond boundaries and surprising us…. We are led by the Spirit into various situations and moments, into meeting points with others, into spaces of encounter and into critical locations of human struggle." (TTL-25/26)

"Authentic Christian witness is not only in *what* we do in mission, but *how* we live out our mission. The church in mission can only be sustained by spiritualities deeply rooted in the Trinity's communion of love." (TTL-29)

Contemporary Witness: Environmental Peacemaking in the Middle East

The same Holy Spirit by whose power Jesus was raised from the dead is the Spirit who brought the world into being at the beginning. We are called to move beyond a narrowly human-centred approach to an understanding of mission which has creation at its heart.

EcoPeace/Friends of the Earth Middle East (FoEME) has been working since 1994 aiming to build inter-community co-operation over environmental issues like water. Water has been a major point of dispute between Israelis and Palestinians. FoEME have been working on this issue to diffuse tension, build peace and nurture a sustainable environment in Israel, the Occupied Territories and Jordan. They work for environmental peacemaking with young people, adults, grassroots organizations and political leaders from all communities. While politics may define borders, environmental issues are not constrained by nationality. FoEME believes that connecting communities through projects and dialogue will create sustainable and healthy ecosystems, as well as help bring peace to the region.

Malek Abulfailat, one of the Palestinian officers in FOEME comments on their cross border work: "When different nationalities and different cultures come together it is inevitable that difficulties arise. It takes time to get to know one another and appreciate these differences. That perhaps, has been the most amazing aspect of my work. Because we have a common goal these cultural issues are of secondary importance. What has become most important is our shared aspiration to improve the situation for our people and make water an equal and undeniable right."

Gidon Bromberg, the Israeli Director, commented: "We hope that the work we do will eventually help facilitate a comprehensive and just water accord between Palestinians and Israelis. We have prepared a model agreement, and we hope that over the next five years we can help raise the standard for what such an agreement could look like, with water justice and environmental sustainability at its heart."[29]

Prayer

Come Holy Spirit
transform with newness
the world that you love
that all creation may
rejoice in freedom with you.

Come Holy Spirit
inspire us to see you
in the places that hide you
and summon us to
witness at your side.

Come Holy Spirit
convert us from death to life
subvert our ways of living
trading, being
that hurt and harm the earth.

Come Holy Spirit
enthuse and renew us
fill us with song
so turning from loss,
we join your dance of life.

---

29. Taken from the following source: http://www.treehugger.com/corporate-responsibility/the-th-interview-gidon-bromberg-friends-of-the-earth-middle-east-part-two.html

Go Holy Spirit
lead and leave us again
push us on our way
send us to our neighbours
and Creation's future day.

Song: Come, Holy Spirit[30]

In Your Local Context: Celebrate, Reflect, Act
Celebrate:
- by organizing a shared meal with neighbours to bless the earth and her Creator
- by going on a prayer walk which marvels at the splendour of God's creation and counters threats to its integrity.

Reflect:
- by imagining a bent reed and inviting the Spirit to come into the places of weakness you harbour or can see around you in your community - to lead you into new life
- on how to shape your lifestyle so that it is sustainable in terms of use of the earth's resources.

Act:
- as you read this material, what do you feel the Spirit is expecting of you? What might you attempt for the flourishing of creation?
- where do you see the Spirit at work in your community and how could you join in?

In Policymaking: Celebrate, Reflect, Act
In the task of setting policy it is important to recognize the leading and the prompting of the Holy Spirit. How can we work professionally while responding to the presence of the Spirit in developing and implementing our policies? Mission has to be lived out in mutuality, reciprocity and interdependence (TTL-45). Therefore we have to ask ourselves if we are

---

30. For words and music, consult the songs chapter at the end of this book.

organized in such a way as to transform power structures and ensure that a true missional partnership with partner/local congregations is reflected.

Celebrate:
- the power of the Holy Spirit – an infinite resource for the fulfillment of Christian mission.
- mutually empowering and life-affirming relationships in the global church.

Reflect:
- to what extent does economic power influence our partnerships? What kind of foot-prints do we make in our partnerships?
- How far are our partnerships and policies shaped by the Spirit to reflect the reality of reconciliation (TTL-30-34)?

Act:
- determine one policy action which will help to bring about changes in power relations and promote mutual accountability?

In Education and Formation: Celebrate, Reflect, Act

Our contemporary context is permeated with a clash of spirits even when it is not evident or acknowledged. The formation of leaders gifted with discernment (TTL-35) is essential if churches are to discover wisdom that leads to truth (TTL-27-28). Missional leaders empty themselves of their privileges for the sake of the disempowered (TTL-33). Through the gift of the Holy Spirit they embrace *metanonia* (repentance) as a process of transformation.

Celebrate:
- leadership formation that embodies and demonstrates the fruit of the Spirit and enables engagement in today's realities in transformative ways.

Reflect:
- how can the Bible be used to develop the spiritual gift of discernment in relation to the life-affirming and life-denying forces at work in our context? See the stories of David and Nathan (II Samuel 12:1-15) and Jesus' healing of the demon-possessed man (Mark 5:1-20).

Act:
- what urgent steps must leaders in your local faith community take to empty themselves of privilege for the sake of the disempowered?
- how can they demonstrate the church's commitment to exposing deceptive powers that deny people fullness of life?

2. Spirit of Liberation: Mission from the Margins

"We believe in God, the Holy Spirit, the Life-giver, who sustains and empowers life and renews the whole creation" (TTL-1). The Holy Spirit empowered Jesus and continues to empower people, within our churches and outside, so that they can participate in God's mission of liberation with a preferential option for the "marginalized."

Bible Study: I Corinthians 1:18-31
The Bible witnesses to a God whose "ways are not human ways" (Isaiah 55: 8-9). God's ways of working appear, on any normal human reckoning, to be weak and foolish. The cross of Jesus is the outstanding example. Paul invites his audience also to consider themselves, chosen to be followers of Jesus not because of their strength or intelligence.

Mission is the mission of God. God is the protagonist and therefore those involved in God's mission have to appreciate that it does not work according to human reckoning. They have to discern, by openness to the Spirit of God, the ways in which God is working.

God's characteristic way of working involves using people perceived to be marginal – the "weak" and the "foolish," the vulgar and the uneducated. The members of the church at Corinth were not impressive by normal human standards but God chose to work through them. In a world where slaves and uneducated people were made to feel worthless, God very often chose them to be the agents of mission and the backbone of the church.

In the past, mission was traditionally understood as being done by the powerful to the powerless, by the rich to the poor, by the privileged to the marginalized. Sadly this has often led to mission being complicit in oppressive and life-denying systems. This text invites us to think instead of the powerless, poor and marginalized as agents of mission. As Jesus put it: "the last shall be first" (Matthew 20:16).

Paul concludes by alluding to Jeremiah 9:23-24: "Let not the wise man boast in his wisdom, let not the mighty man boast in his might, let not the rich man boast in his riches, but let him who boasts boast in this, that I am the Lord who practices steadfast love, justice and righteousness in the earth. For in these things I delight, declares the Lord."

Questions

1. Based on this text, what kind of people might the Spirit of God choose as agents of mission in your context?

2. How can you be part of the movement through which God acts by using the gifts and perspectives of people on the margins of society?

3. What are the structures, systems, values and practices in your local situation – culture, church, society – which are anti-life, anti-community and "marginalizing"?

4. What can be done to change and transform these marginalizing structures, systems, values and practices?

5. What forms of "steadfast love, justice and righteousness" might delight the Lord in your context?

Food for Thought from Together towards Life

"Jesus began his ministry by claiming that to be filled by the Spirit is to liberate the oppressed, to open eyes that are blind, and to announce the coming of God's reign (Luke 4:16-18). He went about fulfilling this mission by opting to be with the marginalized people of his time, not out of paternalistic charity but because their situations testified to the sinfulness of the world, and their yearnings for life pointed to God's purposes." (TTL-36)

"Christian mission has at times been understood and practiced in ways which failed to recognize God's alignment with those consistently pushed to the margins. Therefore, mission from the margins invites the church to re-imagine mission as a vocation from God's Spirit who works for a world where the fullness of life is available for all." (TTL-37)

"People on the margins have agency, and can often see what, from the centre, is out of view. People on the margins, living in vulnerable positions, often know what exclusionary forces are threatening their survival and can best discern the urgency of their struggles; people in positions of privilege have much to learn from the daily struggles of people living in marginal conditions.... Through struggles in and for life, marginalized people are reservoirs of the active hope, collective resistance and perseverance that are needed to remain faithful to the promised reign of God." (TTL-38-39)

"The aim of mission is not simply to move people from the margins to centres of power but to confront those who remain the centre by keeping people on the margins. Instead, churches are called to *transform* power structures." (TTL-40)

"Healing is one of the gifts of the Holy Spirit (I Corinthians 12:9; Acts 3). The Spirit empowers the church for a life-nurturing mission, which includes prayer, pastoral care, and professional health care on the one hand, and prophetic denunciation of the root causes of suffering, transforming structures that dispense injustice and the pursuit of scientific research on the other." (TTL-50)

Contemporary Witness: Malala Yousafzai and Girls' Right to Education

Malala Yousafzai, born 1997, Mingora, Pakistan. Since the age of eleven, this young girl dedicated herself to fight for women's rights and, in a special way, for girls' right to education in opposition to the Taliban. On 9 October 2012, she was shot in the head and neck by Taliban gunmen and gravely injured. Fortunately her life was saved after major surgery.

One day, Malala said: "My purpose is to serve humanity, to serve their rights." And, after the attempt on her life, she said: "Today you can see that I am alive. I can speak, I can see you, I can see everyone. It's just because of the prayers of people. Because all people - men, women, children - all of them have prayed for me. And because of all these prayers God has given me this new life, a second life. And I want to serve. I want to serve the people. I want every girl, every child, to be educated. For that reason, we have organized the Malala Fund."

In Malala, as with many others committed to the same cause of justice, dignity and life for all, we Christians discover the Holy Spirit at work! It is with such people, Christians or not, that the new mission affirmation invites us to collaborate. [TTL-45] Also, her young age confirms the biblical conviction that God chooses the "little ones and the powerless" to carry out his saving and liberating mission.

Prayer

We praise you, O God, for the wonder of your faithfulness. We worship you because you have not abandoned our world but have set about making it new.

We thank you for all that you are doing through our Lord Jesus Christ who came to liberate the oppressed, to open eyes that are blind and to announce the coming of your reign.

Liberator God, *come to set us free.*

We seek your forgiveness for our sins, confessing that:

- We have despised people whom you cherish – the outsiders, the different, the sick, the broken;
- We have made ourselves comfortable in positions of power, careless of those who are excluded;
- We have compromised our commitment to your holy purposes by accommodating your mission to the power systems of this world.

Liberator God, *come to set us free.*

Transform us, living God, that we might be agents of your justice, peace, healing and reconciliation. Grant that we might follow the way of Jesus who came not to be served but to serve. Take us to difficult places and grant us the courage to live out the reality of your reign.

Liberator God, *come to set us free.*

All for your glory and in the name of our living Lord and Saviour, Jesus Christ.

Song: God of Life

Celebrate, Reflect, Act
Celebrate:
- The ways of God who "has brought down the powerful from their thrones and lifted up the lowly; who has filled the hungry with good things and sent the rich away empty" (Luke 1:52-53).

- Men and women of yesterday and today, irrespective of their age, religion, race, social class who, like Malala, have dedicated themselves to the service of the marginalized, to the point of risking their lives.

Reflect:
- What motivates and empowers such people to fulfill their mission?
- Where are the margins in your local context?

Act:
- Identify concrete actions against marginalization that can be taken locally to make a difference in the life of the whole community.
- Identify steps that can show solidarity with people marginalized by exclusionary forces working within the global economy.

In Policymaking: Celebrate, Reflect, Act

It is important to take account of the voices of silence and discomfort which cry out on behalf of those of us who are oppressed or excluded. How then can margin and centre come together, listen to each other and work with each another? While establishing new partnerships churches and organizations need to be more relevant to the increasing numbers of migrant communities. It is time to re-imagine identity and gain an identity in terms of partnership within the world-wide church.

Celebrate:
- the voices of those who raise a prophetic voice and make us uncomfortable.

Reflect:
- how do we understand our own social location (as organization and as individual) in relation to the issues of margins and centre?
- what responses are needed to the impact of migration on societies and churches?
- In the light of the power issue of "margins" and "centre," how do we evaluate rapidly changing financial capacities of churches and organizations in both North and South? How can our resources be used in such a way that they strengthen equality and mutuality?

Act:
- determine one way in which you will adjust the use of financial resources so that they do not prevent but rather strengthen mission from the margins.

In Education and Formation: Celebrate, Reflect, Act

Genuine "liberation" (TTL-100) is an indispensable gift of the Spirit that must embrace all creation. In many societies liberation movements that promised socio-economic transformation have failed to deliver. People experience increased oppression and marginalization. The exercise of good missional leadership creates space, invites and empowers others to come in and express their gifts (TTL-47). This calls into question blind allegiance to one's identity and ethnicity because this can lead us to embrace forces that deny life.

Celebrate:
- examples of missional formation of leaders (TTL-45) characterized by "mutuality, reciprocity and interdependence."

Reflect:
- given today's widespread cynicism in relation to liberation movements and political institutions, how may we foster the kind of leadership which is marked by mutuality, reciprocity, interdependence and empowerment?

Act:
- identify three practical ways in which those who live on the margins can be empowered for engagement in missional leadership?

3. Spirit of Community: Church on the Move

Mission is the very being of the church. The church exists by mission, just as the fire exists by burning. If it does not engage itself in mission, then it ceases to exist as church. The church is a pilgrim people, always on the move – literally and metaphorically – in a world which is only a temporary

home. Practically, mission and unity belong together. The church, therefore, is called to genuine unity which always entails inclusivity and respect
for others. Empowered and energized by the indwelling of the Holy Spirit,
the church will be able to move forward as a community of believers.

Bible Study: Acts 15:6-21

A question churches often have to face is whether to remain in their comfort zone or to become a church on the move. A decisive event in the story
of the early church was the Council held at Jerusalem and described in
Acts 15.

A dramatically new situation had arisen in Antioch where a church
had emerged composed of both Jews and Gentiles who had come to faith
in Jesus Christ. To traditionally-minded Jews this was unthinkable. They
were willing to allow Gentiles to become church members but only on the
condition that they first became Jews – by being circumcised and accept-
ing the obligation to keep the Mosaic law. Some of these conservative Jewish Christians came to Antioch to put their case to the new converts. Paul
and Barnabas resisted their argument, insisting that faith in Jesus was the
only condition of church membership and that Jewish identity was not
required. The result was deadlock and the only way to get an authoritative
decision was to appeal to church HQ in Jerusalem.

When the Council met in Jerusalem, a powerful argument advanced
by Peter was his observation that the Gentile believers received the Holy
Spirit in just the same way as the Jewish Christians. This made it clear that
God did not make any distinction. Regardless of background, those who
had faith in Jesus Christ belonged to the church on the same basis. With
the debate finely balanced, people looked to James, the brother of Jesus
and someone who was highly respected for his strong faith and sound
character. He himself was a rigorous observer of the Jewish law. When
he came down in favour of admitting Jews and Gentiles to church membership on the same basis of God's free grace in Christ, received by faith
alone, this was decisive for the outcome of the Council. It also accepted
the guidelines he suggested to make for integrity of faith and life, and
allow for fellowship between Jewish and Gentile believers. The Council's

decision opened the way for the church to be "on the move" throughout the Gentile world.

Questions

1. What opportunities do you see in your context for people who have previously been separated to come together in the life of the church?

2. What religious and cultural conditioning might be at work in your life to hinder recognition of God's Spirit working in new and unexpected ways?

3. In your context what factors prevent the church from being united? What guidelines might help to overcome causes of division and to attain the unity for which Christ prayed?

4. Doubts about whether non-Jews could be accepted into church membership could have been a barrier obstructing the onward movement of the church in the first century. What barriers threaten to hinder onward movement today?

Food for Thought from Together towards Life

"The relationship between church and mission is very intimate because the same Spirit of Christ who empowers the church in mission is also the life of the church. At the same time as he sent the church into the world, Jesus Christ breathed the Holy Spirit into the church (John 20:19-23). Therefore the church exists by mission, just as a fire exists by burning. If it does not engage in mission, it ceases to be the church." (TTL-57)

Mission is not a project of expanding churches but of the church embodying God's salvation in this world. Out of this follows a dynamic understanding of the apostolicity of the church: apostolicity is not only safeguarding the faith of the church through the ages but also participating in the apostolate. Thus the churches mainly and foremost need to be missionary churches. (TTL-58)

Churches can be a place of refuge for migrant communities; they can also be intentional focal points for inter-cultural engagement. The churches are called to be one to serve God's mission beyond ethnic and cultural boundaries and ought to create multi-cultural ministry and mission as a concrete expression of common witness in diversity. (TTL-70)

God's hospitality calls us to move beyond binary notions of culturally dominant groups as hosts, and migrant and minority peoples as guests. Instead, in God's hospitality, God is host and we are all invited by the Spirit to participate with humility and mutuality in God's mission. (TTL-71)

Contemporary Witness: Church on the Border

It remains one of the fundamental tasks of the church's mission to break down the walls that divide, alienate, exclude, discriminate, and dehumanize. Some seek to breakdown these barriers in creative ways along the US-Mexican border. One community decided to have a volleyball game at the border with respective teams on each side. Another held a picnic and shared food between the holes in the border fence. And various communities hold Eucharistic liturgies where both the altar and the congregation are, at the same time, joined together and kept apart by the border wall. Needless to say, sharing the peace at these liturgies is a very moving experience. A Eucharist at the border is not simply a political statement but an eschatological and a social one, emphasizing not only that the walls will come down when Christ comes again but that we already share a unity because of who we are as the body of Christ.

Migration, in the end, is not simply a social, political, and economic matter but a theological event and a spiritual issue. We deport something of our souls when we fail to welcome the stranger. Not only do the walls of self-security not keep us truly safe, but in the process, as we neglect the vulnerability of others but we lose touch with our own vulnerability in this earthly sojourn and, in the process, forget our interconnectedness with the body of Christ. Our fundamental identity rests in the end not on the

creed of a nation but on whom we are as a pilgrim people and our movement outward in mission to strangers in need.[31]

—Fr Daniel G. Groody, csc

Prayer

Holy and everlasting God, we worship you for you are love. We marvel
that you unceasingly pour out your love into the life of our world. And we
are moved as your love opens our hearts and we discover what it is to love
one another.

God of community, *make us Christ's body.*

We praise you that your mission in the world has drawn people together
to form the life of the church. We give thanks for your Holy Spirit who
unfailingly empowers the church for mission.

God of community, *make us Christ's body.*

Forgive us, O God,

- For the pride and hatred which has brought disunity to the life of
  your church;
- For our absorption with our own petty concerns and our neglect of
  your mission agenda;
- For all the times that we stuck with people with whom we were
  comfortable when you were calling us to step out to welcome the
  stranger.

God of community, *make us Christ's body.*

Grant that we may know the empowering and energizing that comes from
your Holy Spirit:

- Giving us courage to take new initiatives so that the life of your
  church will be relevant to the people of our time and place;

---

31. Fr Daniel G. Groody, csc, *Address to the Assembly of the International Association for
Mission Studies* Toronto, August 2012.

- Opening our hearts to people, from near or far, with whom we belong together in the life of the one church;
- Creating imagination so that we may discover new ways to form friendships, struggle for justice, and act in service.

God of community, *make us Christ's body.*

For we bring our prayers in his precious name. Amen

Song: Jesus, where can we find you?

Celebrate, Reflect, Act

Celebrate:

- the unity of the church, even when imperfectly realized. How beautiful it is when sisters and brothers dwell together in unity (Ps. 133:1).
- new forms of church life coming into being in our time.

Reflect:

- on what would have to change in the life of your church to make it more welcoming to migrants who have come from elsewhere?
- on what your local church could do to participate more fully in the life of the church worldwide?

Act:

- take the next steps needed to bring greater unity to the outreach of the churches in your area.
- identify a situation, local or global, where justice and peace are lacking and start taking action as an advocate for justice.

In Policymaking: Celebrate, Reflect, Act

Mission is about embodying God's salvation in the world. Thus it invites people to become a part of the Christian community. How can this be translated into missional policies, which provide quality nurture so that people live as disciples? In the light of global migration, how can we embrace migrants both locally and internationally as partners in mission? How can programmatic activities of the agencies be life-affirming and respectful of creation and its resources?

Celebrate:
- the spirit of life as a criterion for relating the gospel to wisdom traditions and other faiths in a spirit of cooperation.

- the emergence of world Christianity during the past century as churches have been formed in many different parts of the earth.

Reflect:
- how can churches accommodate renewal within their structures when the fresh expression is different from the dominant style of worship and theology?

- In an effort to professionalize development work there may be pressure to loosen its connection to Christian roots. How can Christian identity and professionalism be reconciled?

Act:
- determine one new partnership strategy which will take account of the impact of migration in today's world.

- What identity and shape should mission and development bodies ideally and practically have in the future in order to remain relevant for the life of the church and the world?

In Education and Formation: Celebrate, Reflect, Act
The new landscape highlights the impact of globalization and migration on nations. This calls for intercultural missional formation of leaders (TTL-75-76). New guidelines are needed to facilitate authentic engagement in evangelism (TTL-90). It is critical today to be life-affirming and to foster integrity in Christian witness.

Celebrate:

- ecumenical convictions that affirm common witness and life-giving mission in a multi-religious world?

Reflect:

- while cherishing our particular church identity can we identify ways in which we use it to alienate and exclude others?

Act:

- what steps can be taken to deploy the gifts and capacities of groups often excluded from ecclesial leadership, such as children, youth, women, migrant, indigenous, disabled?

4. Spirit of Pentecost: Good News for All

Since the Day of Pentecost the Holy Spirit has inspired people to proclaim the good news of Jesus Christ, inviting others to personal conversion and a new life of discipleship. The true agent of evangelism is the Holy Spirit. We are invited to discern where the Spirit is at work and to share our faith with humility, respect and confidence.

Bible Study: Acts 10:1-48.

This story lets us see how both Cornelius and Peter were transformed by the Holy Spirit through their encounter with one another. Though Cornelius, an officer in the Roman army, had never before heard of Jesus he was a person of deep spirituality. Though Peter, a devout 1st century Jew, had never thought that Gentiles could be baptized, he was open to the new thing which the Holy Spirit was doing.

Cornelius was a Roman soldier at a time when Roman rule held sway. Roman army officers bestrode the world, and were regarded with awe, respect and fear. A centurion appointed to a strategic centre like Caesarea would be battle-hardened, dependable, efficient. More often than not, he would be contemptuous toward local religion and culture. Cornelius was different in this respect: he was attracted by the Jewish faith – belief in one

God and maintenance of a pure ethic. His deepening spirituality prepared him for the encounter he would have with Peter.

To appreciate where Peter was coming from we have to understand how deep lay the distinction between Jew and Gentile in the minds of first-century Jews. Strict Jews would order their lives so that they did not have any social interaction with the Gentiles. Their whole project as God's chosen people was to keep themselves pure and avoid the contamination which contact with Gentiles would entail. The big eye-opener for Peter was the realization that the Old Testament food laws, one of the bastions of Jewish exclusivism, were now being set aside – in the light of the coming of Jesus. This realization prepared him for the moment when the Holy Spirit fell upon the Gentiles gathered in the house of Cornelius and there was no reason for them not to be baptized.

Questions

1. What kind of faith did Cornelius have before he heard about Jesus?

2. In what way was Peter "converted" when he was praying on the roof at Joppa?

3. What points did Peter emphasize when he made his speech at the house of Cornelius?

4. What was the role of the Holy Spirit in the conversion of those who heard Peter speak?

Food for Thought from Together towards Life

"Evangelism is sharing the good news both in word and action. Evangelizing through verbal proclamation or preaching of the gospel is profoundly biblical. However, if our words are not consistent with our actions, our evangelism is inauthentic." (TTL-86)

"Authentic evangelism is grounded in humility and respect for all, and flourishes in the context of dialogue.... Evangelism, therefore, inspires the building of inter-personal and community relationships. Such authentic relationships are often best nourished in local faith communities, and based on local cultural contexts. Christian witness is as much by our presence as by our words." (TTL-89)

"The Holy Spirit works in mysterious ways, and we do not fully understand the workings of the Spirit in other faith traditions. We acknowledge that there is inherent value and wisdom in diverse life-giving spiritualities. Therefore, authentic mission makes the "other" a partner in, not an "object" of mission." (TTL-93)

"God is there before we come (Acts 17) and our task is not to bring God along, but to witness to the God who is already there. Dialogue provides for an honest encounter where each party brings to the table all that they are in an open, patient and respectful manner." (TTL-94)

Contemporary Witness: St Paul's Mission of India

Shivaji (not his real name) is one of the marginalized people who recently came to faith in Jesus Christ through the work of St Paul's Mission of India, the missionary arm of the Malankara Jacobite Syrian Orthodox Church in India. I met him when I went to our mission field in Bihar for the consecration of a new chapel. Our missionaries there and other friends introduced him to me and told me that Shivaji until recently meant terror in the village. In fact, he had spent seven years in prison for the crime of chopping the head of a farmer during a feud. He was released from prison only a couple of years ago.

After he was released, the Hindu religious fundamentalists in the region used him to terrorize our missionaries who have been working among the most vulnerable and backward sections of the village. Several of our evangelists and believers who accepted Christ and joined the church were severely persecuted under the leadership of Shivaji. Now the same Shivaji who used to torture our missionaries and the faithful has been converted and has accepted Christ as his liberator. Today, no one dares to come and trouble the mission work because of Shivaji's presence there! His wife came to Christ first and through her, Shivaji also accepted the gospel of Christ as his source of liberation.

His presence and participation in the Holy Liturgy of the Eucharist was a profound experience for me. I was spiritually moved when I shared the Holy Elements with Shivaji. The mission work of St. Paul's Mission of India in Bihar which led to the conversion of Shivaji and several others constitutes what I prefer to term "liturgy before liturgy." The fruits of this "liturgy before liturgy" made the actual liturgy much more meaningful. To me, Shivaji represents St. Paul who like Shivaji used to persecute Christ and Christians before he was caught by the love of Christ. Shivaji, "the St. Paul of St. Paul's Mission of India" in Bihar is being used as a great source of inspiration and challenge.

Here, it was not just Shivaji who has been liberated, but through him and the mission work, the church has also been challenged to come out of its casteist mindset and power structures so that the church can be a true manifestation of God's reign on earth, everyone being treated with equality and dignity. The Syrian Orthodox Church in India due to its "upper caste" consciousness and attitudes, inherited from the caste Hindu mindset, has tended to be an exclusive and clannish community, not enthusiastic about outreach evangelism as this would bring the "outcaste" people such as Dalits into the church fold and therefore would unsettle the caste structure of the church. The conversion of people like Shivaji is bringing a mini-revolution as caste walls within the church structures are beginning to crack due to the power of Christ's gospel. The work of St. Paul's Mission of India is proving to be a "double edged sword" - it liberates not only "the evangelized" (Dalits and Adivasis who are being freed from the clutches of caste slavery and socio-economic marginalization) but also "the evangelists" (the Syrian Orthodox Church which is being challenged about its caste structures and mentality).

—Metropolitan Geevarghese Coorilos Nalunnakkal

Prayer

Glory be to you, living God, for your mighty acts of salvation. We praise you that through the coming, the suffering, the dying and the rising again of our Lord Jesus Christ you have acted to bring salvation to us and to our world.

What else could we do, O Lord, *but declare your mighty acts?*

We marvel that you have chosen such frail instruments as us to take the good news to our friends and neighbours. We praise you that the message remains powerful today to transform individuals and communities.

What else could we do, O Lord, *but declare your mighty acts?*

Forgive us, O God,
- For the times we have been timid or afraid and have failed to make known your gospel;
- For the times when our actions belied our words as we failed to live in a way that is true to Jesus;
- For the times we have been aggressive or coercive, failing to show the respect which honours your name.

What else could we do, O Lord, *but declare your mighty acts?*

Give us courage, O God
- To share our lives and beliefs openly and respectfully with those who do not hold our faith, learning from them and sharing with them;
- To proclaim the gospel and seek the partnership of the poor, the dispossessed and the despized, being shaped by the way they see things;
- To be open to the challenge brought to our own limited perspective by those who understand the good news from a different cultural perspective.

What else could we do, O Lord, *but declare your mighty acts?*

So we bring these our prayers in the name of our risen Lord, even Jesus Christ. *Amen*

Song: A ivangeli ya famba (The Gospel is going)

Celebrate, Reflect, Act

Celebrate:
- the journey you have made to faith in the living God.
- the journeys made by all who put their trust in Christ today.

Reflect:
- on what you can do to ensure that your evangelism is grounded in humility and respect for all.
- on ways in which the gospel affirms, challenges or transforms your particular culture.

Act:
- identify opportunities you have to openly express to others your faith in Christ.
- identify opportunities you have to share your life with someone of another faith and to develop mutually respectful dialogue.

In Policymaking: Celebrate, Reflect, Act

Churches and agencies need to accommodate renewal coming from the moving of the Spirit and voices from the margin. There has to be a balance in policymaking between the demand for effectiveness and professionalism and the need to develop friendships and relationships which can take into account the need for renewal. Renewal of life, as a prompting of the Spirit, can put a strain on relationships when people become followers of Christ and are excluded from their own community. What can the responses be in cases of conversion?

Celebrate:
- the movement of sending and receiving which has taken the good news of Jesus Christ in its different dimensions to many new contexts around the world.

Reflect:
- how can mission bodies develop their programmatic activities in such a way that other religions are respected while, at the same time, the gospel is communicated in an authentic way?
- if "life" is a criterion for discerning the Spirit of God, how can this strengthen cooperation with those of other faiths and secular organizations who want to affirm life and promote reconciliation?

Act:
- take one action which aims to make the renewal of your policy and programmes open to the leading of the Spirit.

In Education and Formation: Celebrate, Reflect, Act

Transformative missional formation recognizes that the *missio Dei*, being in mission, is greater than the loyalty to denominational and local identities. Identity is a gift from God, which needs to be celebrated and explored, resulting in what is life-giving to all.

Celebrate:
- all initiatives worldwide to overcome disunity among the churches and to offer a common witness.

Reflect:
- how can the gospel be proclaimed with integrity in a world disappointed by Christians?
- Given that we ourselves are guests in God's kingdom, how may we be welcoming and hospitable toward those from whom we have been separated and alienated but who are also responding to the invitation of God?

Act:
- identify the elements needed in leadership formation to ensure that outreach and proclamation are evangelism and not proselytism?

Conclusion: "Receive the Holy Spirit"

Following the crucifixion of Jesus we are told that, "the doors of the house where the disciples had met were locked for fear of the Jews" (John 20:19). In today's world disciples of Jesus can find many reasons to be afraid. We could easily be tempted to lock the doors and concern ourselves with self-preservation. The gospel, however, leads in a different direction. Jesus came and stood among them saying: "Peace be with you. As the Father has sent me so I send you" (John 20:21). Hiding behind locked doors was not their calling. Instead they were sent on a mission modeled after the mission of Jesus. Finally, he breathed on them and said, "Receive the Holy Spirit" (John 20:22). This practical guide to the new World Council of Churches mission affirmation *Together towards Life* has highlighted some of the main ways in which this reality might take effect in today's context.

Neither the affirmation nor the guide is intended to be a terminus. On the contrary, they aim to stimulate movement to take Christian mission forward into the future. The Commission for World Mission and Evangelism already has plans to hold consultations during 2014 to develop further thinking on the implications of the new mission affirmation for policymaking and for leadership formation. It is not the intention, however, that initiative should lie only with the Commission. On the contrary, the aim is that *Together towards Life* will stimulate a movement of missionary thinking and action which will re-energize the churches to engage the world of the 21st century in the power of the Holy Spirit.

To give expression to this movement you are invited to share your own reflections, experiences and actions as you respond to the new mission affirmation. This can be done either by posting on the Facebook page of the World Council of Churches Commission for World Mission and Evangelism: *WCC/mission and Evangelism (CWME)* or writing to the Commission at *150 route de Ferney, 1211 Geneva 2, Switzerland.* Your contributions will extend and deepen the fresh understanding of mission amidst changing landscapes which has been articulated in the new mission affirmation. Only when it is generating fresh missionary movement and inspiring fresh missionary engagement will the document have fulfilled its task. In this you, along with many others, have a key role to play. The Commission looks forward with keen anticipation to receiving your contribution.

Songs

Come, Holy Spirit

Theme for the CWME, Athens, 2005

Sister Céline Monteiro, India
Harm. Horacio Vivares, Argentina

Original English text : CWME, 2005 . Music: Sister Celine Monteiro. Harmonization: Horacio Vivares.
Spanish, French, German adaptations: Simei Monteiro © WCC-COE. 150, Route de Ferney, CH-1211, Geneva 2, Switzerland

God of life

Theme, World Council of Churches
10th Assembly

Geonyong Lee, Korea

God of life, God of life, lead us to jus - tice,

lead us to jus - tice and your peace, and your peace.

Jesus, Where Can We Find You?

Doreen Potter: Jamaica

1. Je-sus, where can we find you in our world to - day?
2. Je-sus, in hand of the heal - er can we feel you there?
1. Dans no - tre mon - de d'au - jour - d'hui trou - vons - nous Jé - sus?
2. Dans le com - bat du mé - de - cin vo - yons - nous Jé - sus?

Je - sus, where can we find you In - car - nate Word to - day?
Je - sus, in word of the preach - er can we hear you there?
Ver - be de Dieu de - ve - nu chair, où le trou - ves - tu?
Dans les mots du pré - di - ca - teur, le ren - con - tres - tu?

Refrain

Look at your broth-er be - side you; look at your sis-ter be - side you. Look! Lis-ten! Care!
Tour-ne tes yeux vers le pro-chain, en-tends son cri sur ton che - min. Vois! Ai-me! Sers!

3. Jesus, in mind of the leader
can we know you there?
Jesus, in aims of the planner
can we find you there?

4. Jesus, in thought of the artist
can we sense you there?
Jesus, in work of the builder †
can we see you there?

5. Jesus, in face of the famished
can we see you there?
Jesus, in face of the prisoner †
can we see you there?

6. Jesus, in faces of children
can we see you there?
Jesus, in all of creation
can we find you there?

3. Dans les calculs du chef d'Ètat
sentons-nous Jésus?
Dans les verdicts des magistrats
le dÈcouvres-tu?

4. Peintre, musicien ou sculpteur,
connaÔt-il Jésus?
Dans l'oeuvre de l'entrepreneur
perÂois-tu JÈsus?

5. En secourant les affamÈs
voyons-nous Jésus?
En visitant les prisonniers
servons-nous Jésus?

6. Jésus, dans un regard d'enfant,
te saluons-nous?
Dans le monde entier en tourment,
te confessons-nous?

A ivangeli ya famba

Trad. Xitswa, Mozambique

* insert names of countries or continents, e.g. India, America, Jamaica, UK, etc.

(The Gospel is going (is going) all over the world.
We will take it to *Africa, India, America, Jamaica, UK, etc.)

(Das Evangelium umrundet (umrundet) die Welt.
Wir bezeugen es in *Afrika, Indien, Amerika, Jamaica, UK, usw.)

(L'Evangile parcourt (parcourt) le monde.
Nous l'emmènerons en *Afrique, en Inde, en Amérique, en Jamaïque, au Royaume-Uni, etc.)

(El Evangelio va (va) por todo el mundo.
Lo llevaremos a *Africa, a India, a América, a Jamaica, al Reino Unido, etc.)